THE EVERYTHING KIDS' SPELLING BOOK

Spell yo
S-U-C-

Shelley Gallowa

Aadam

AVON, MA

DEMC

PUBLISHER Karen Cooper

DIRECTOR OF ACQUISITIONS AND INNOVATION Paula Munier

MANAGING EDITOR, EVERYTHING SERIES Lisa Laing

COPY CHIEF Casey Ebert

ACQUISITIONS EDITOR Katie McDonough

ASSOCIATE DEVELOPMENT EDITOR Elizabeth Kassab

EDITORIAL ASSISTANT Hillary Thompson

An Everything® Series Book.
Everything® and everything.com® are registered trademarks of F+W Media, Inc.

Published by Adams Media, a division of F+W Media, Inc.
57 Littlefield Street, Avon, MA 02322. U.S.A.
www.adamsmedia.com

ISBN 10: 1-59869-754-4
ISBN 13: 978-1-59869-754-4

Printed in the United States of America.

J I H G F E D C B A

This publication is designed to provide accurate and authoritative information with regard to
the subject matter covered. It is sold with the understanding that the publisher is not engaged
in rendering legal, accounting, or other professional advice. If legal advice or other expert
assistance is required, the services of a competent professional person should be sought.
—From a *Declaration of Principles* jointly adopted by a Committee of the
American Bar Association and a Committee of Publishers and Associations

Many of the designations used by manufacturers and sellers to distinguish their products are
claimed as trademarks. When those designations appear in this book and Adams Media was
aware of a trademark claim, the designations have been printed with initial capital letters.

Interior illustrations by Kurt Dolber.
Puzzles by Scot Ritchie.

This book is available at quantity discounts for bulk purchases.
For information, please call 1-800-289-0963.

Dedication

This book is dedicated to my
son, Arthur. Over the years, the
two of us have certainly spent
hours getting ready for spelling
tests! Looking back, I'd have to
say I'd do it all again.

Acknowledgments

I'd like to thank my agent,
Mary Sue Seymour, for encour-
aging me to try my hand at
nonfiction. I would be remiss
if I didn't also thank my many
teaching colleagues and the
administrators who mentored
me in the many schools in
which I taught. Being a good
teacher is difficult. Being a
wonderful teacher who gives a
lot of herself year after year is
extremely hard to do. I've been
blessed to know many such
men and women. Thanks again
for sharing your expertise.

Contents

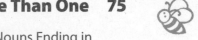

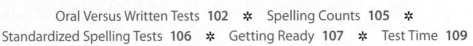

Introduction

Spelling! Has there ever been a more complicated or dreaded subject? Sometimes it's amazing that anyone is able to read, let alone learn to spell, so many words in the English language! It can be really frustrating to learn one way to spell words just to realize that there are a whole lot more words that don't want to follow the rules!

The English language is a true mixture of other languages. Today, many words in our language come from other countries, such as Mexico, Spain, France, and Greece. Many, many English words also have origins in Latin. Champion spellers study other languages to be super spellers. But for the rest of us, sometimes it's just a matter of being familiar with some of the root words.

Perhaps instead of worrying about its necessity, it would be better to think of how being a good speller can help you succeed in a variety of subjects. Spelling words correctly can help almost anyone focus on the subject at hand. It's a whole lot easier to write a letter to your aunt or a paper about airplanes if you don't stumble over every word you want to use. This book offers an incredible array of activities to help you spell better. Just because something is important does not mean learning to do it well will give you a headache!

By studying various ways to learn spelling rules and putting them into practice, you'll be able to learn more about how you learn. Maybe you like to draw pictures. Maybe you like to sing songs. Maybe you like to do puzzles. This book will show you how to study spelling in all of these ways.

You can apply some of these spelling skills and games to other subjects. If you learn to spell by looking at a word, covering it up to memorize it, writing it down, and then checking your progress, you might find that learning vocabulary for other subjects may work for you, too. Maybe that method will help you learn the fifty states and capitals—and their correct spellings!

Finally, studying spelling doesn't have to be boring. Use *The Everything® Kids' Spelling Book* as a resource to help you to succeed. Who knows? Maybe you'll also find it to be a fun way to practice your words and to learn a new game. No matter what, take a deep breath, put on your thinking cap, and challenge yourself.

Dear Readers,

Spelling was never an easy subject for me in school. In order to succeed, I began to try other ways to learn to spell. I made up games and poems and created spelling guides to help me, and I learned how to spell in spite of the many obstacles I faced.

During my years as a teacher, I met many smart kids who had a hard time spelling correctly. There wasn't one single method of studying or spelling that worked best. I learned various methods to teach and practice spelling. Those experiences led to this book.

In many ways, learning to spell is like competing in a race. There are many ways to reach the finish line, but the goal is essentially the same—to feel satisfaction from completing a job well done. Though you may find it easiest to progress through this book in order, it is certainly not the only way to use it. You may want to use this book as a reference when you are searching for spelling games or puzzles. You might find this book useful when looking for additional ways to master a particular spelling rule. Finally, there are a variety of spelling lists throughout the book.

Spelling is certainly not a new subject in school; however, it remains a key part of education. Spelling well allows you to communicate better, express your ideas more completely, and succeed in other subject areas. Best of luck to you!

Shelley Galloway Sabga

Chapter 1

Getting Started

How Do You Learn?

Let's face it—spelling is part of our everyday life. Whether you need to write a quick note to your mom or an essay about geography for your teacher, spelling comes into play. Being able to spell well lets you concentrate on what you want to say instead of how you want to say it. However, that doesn't mean learning how to spell is easy. Many, many very smart kids will tell you that spelling well is a challenge for them.

It's Tougher Than It Seems

People who had trouble with spelling will tell you that they overcame their difficulties by coming up with different ways to make up for their struggles. Some might tell you that their tricks did not come easily, but most will say that once they found methods that worked, they used them often—and they may still use them today. With this book as a resource, you will have a number of spelling strategies at your fingertips to assist you whenever you run into difficulty. If spelling becomes less frustrating for you, then that will be a reason to celebrate!

How Do You Study?

Take a moment to think about how you study best. What were two things you have done that were especially helpful? Plan to incorporate those strategies when you study spelling.

BETTER LETTER

A lot of words look similar at first, but if you change a letter they take on a whole new meaning. Can you see what these words would become if you replaced a letter with an L in each one?

In the word **stack** change one letter to describe a piece of celery.

_ _ _ _ _

Replace one letter in **song** to describe something that is not short.

_ _ _ _

Replace the double letters to make **berry** something everyone has.

_ _ _ _ _

Change an r in **order** to describe somebody who is not as young as you.

_ _ _ _ _

Change a letter in **hike** to describe something you enjoy.

_ _ _ _

Change one letter in **decay** to describe something that makes you wait.

_ _ _ _ _

If you change one letter in **foot**, you get somebody acting silly.

_ _ _ _

Long Ago and Far, Far Away . . .

Years ago, everyone thought there was only one way to learn spelling words—by writing them over and over and over. Unfortunately, that didn't always help. Some people only got hand and finger cramps, and they still couldn't spell! At best, it was boring; at worst, it was painful. Luckily, there are much more fun ways to practice your spelling. That is what this book is all about.

A good starting point is to discover just what tools you need in your personal study toolbox to become a super speller. Like having a hammer at your fingertips makes hanging a picture a whole lot easier, having good study habits will make you a better speller.

There's More Than One Way . . .

You might already know which study methods work best for you. Perhaps you've already had to memorize facts for social studies or science quizzes in school. Think back to how you studied. How did you learn the information? Was it from having a parent quiz you orally? Did you make flashcards and play memory or matching games? Did you write notes or maybe reread the chapter that the test was on? Maybe you needed a different type of learning tool. Maybe learning the facts to the rhythm of a nursery rhyme or popular song helped. Perhaps drawing a picture or organizing a timeline to illustrate facts helped you.

Learning Styles

People learn in ways that are most comfortable for them. These learning styles don't end when a person gets out of school, either. In fact, a lot of people tend to do jobs based on

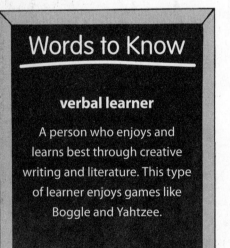

Words to Know

verbal learner

A person who enjoys and learns best through creative writing and literature. This type of learner enjoys games like Boggle and Yahtzee.

their learning style when they get older. That makes sense. If a person learns by doing, perhaps he'll be a chemist or an inventor or a chef. If she learns best by reading, she might become a writer or a researcher. A musician probably always liked making up songs or putting information to rhythm. All of us don't learn in just one way, either. We can be strong in several areas. Have you ever given some thought to how you like to study or learn? What are your talents? Do you have an idea of what you might want to do in the future?

Suggested Supplies

Let's get organized. The items in the following list might help you do some of these activities or chart your progress. If you have these items around the house, gather them up and put them in a spelling corner or a spelling box. If you don't, pick these materials up next time you are at the store. They are not terribly expensive, but they will come in handy.

- **A lined flip chart.** These flip charts can be found at office supply stores. They have a spiral top and can be hung on the wall or put on a stand. These charts are helpful to list words you are learning or words you've mastered, or to organize your thoughts. You can make your own flip chart with a few white poster boards. Draw lines on them with black marker. If you laminate them or cover them with clear contact paper, you can easily wash off your words with some window cleaner and make new lists any time you want.
- **Markers.** I bet you already have these. If not, get some thick markers so you can make big, clear letters. Don't forget to have some dark colors, like black, blue, and green. You want words that will be easy to see. If you

Words to Know

logical learner

A person who enjoys problem solving and likes step-by-step directions. Games such as checkers or chess appeal to this person.

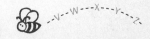

MISTAKES TO A-V-O-I-D

Remain Calm!

Sometimes when you begin to study, do you get overwhelmed by attempting to tackle everything at once? Try not to let a huge list of words or a big assignment get to you. Just take it a few words at a time. Plan to learn five to seven words really well at one time. You'll have a better chance of success.

plan to erase your work on a laminated sheet, make sure the markers are washable. Crayons will also work just fine.

- **Highlighters.** These are great tools. With highlighters, you can highlight words in books, magazines, or newspapers. You can also color-code words to show your level of progression. Get some highlighters in at least two or three colors.
- **Paper.** You'll need lots of paper. Put a variety of sheets, such as lined paper, white copy paper, and construction paper, in a file folder.
- **Books or magazines.** Get some books you can read easily and a variety of magazines that you can cut up.
- **Index cards.** These are useful for organizing words, making flashcards, and doing other projects. It doesn't matter what size or color they are.
- **Pencils.** Obviously, you're going to be writing a lot. Make sure you have a good supply with good erasers!

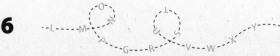

High-Frequency Word Lists

Teachers have drawn up a list of the 100 most commonly used words in the written language. You might already know some of the words. Becoming familiar with this list will help you when deciding which words to concentrate on learning to spell. Appendix A contains many of the words in this list divided by grade level.

Let's look a little more closely at the high-frequency word list. For first graders, some high-frequency words are **the**, **and**, and **to**. These are all important, highly used words. But they're also difficult to define, right? It would be very hard to try to tell someone what **the** means. It's also impossible to draw a picture to illustrate the word **the**. Don't worry! Help is here! Here are a couple of ways to master the list:

- Have a parent write the words on a chart. Highlight the words in yellow as you begin to study them.

  - Highlight over the yellow in blue when you have mastered the words. This will make the words green, and they will be your GO-to words! You know them! Hooray!
  - If there are words that you are continually having trouble learning, highlight them in pink. They can be your stop, look, and listen words, just like at a traffic light. These words can also be words that you might master and then forget soon after. The pink highlighter can serve as your warning light.

- Pick twenty words on the list to begin studying. Write them on your flip chart, poster board, or notebook paper. Read each word out loud. Being able to read and write words is what spelling is all about. Now, pick a paragraph

Headline Headache

Double Vision

What do you think of when you see the headline "Big Ugly Woman Wins Beauty Pageant"? You're probably wondering what the other contestants in that beauty pageant looked like! But it all makes sense when you learn that the winner was from a city named Big Ugly in West Virginia. Here are some other headlines that have different meanings depending on how you read them. Can you guess what they are?

March Planned for Next August

_____

_____

Stolen Painting Found by Tree

_____

_____

Burglar Steals Clock, Faces Time

_____

_____

Eye Drops Off Shelf

_____

_____

  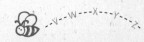

What's the Frequency?

The words that are used the most often in the English language are **a**, **I**, **and**, and **the**. Choose a paragraph in today's newspaper. How many of these words did you find? How many times were they used?

in a magazine or newspaper. Using a highlighter, practice locating and highlighting any spelling words that you can find in that paragraph. How many of your spelling words did you find? You'll find some words so often that you'll know exactly why they are called high-frequency words!

- Use a shoebox and index cards to keep track of your words. Write down your spelling words on the cards, and then have them handy when you study. Using index cards can also help if you're the type of learner who likes to draw or use your hands to remember information.

Ways to Practice

Throughout this book, you will find all different kinds of spelling stumpers and sections about tackling the spelling of unfamiliar words. You'll look at words that are contractions, pronouns, homonyms, and synonyms. As you go through the book, you may want to get an idea about how to study and practice them. Here are a variety of ideas and activities that you might want to try.

- Put your words in ABC order.
- Write each word from your list three times, each in a different color. How many different combinations of colors can you come up with?
- Instead of scrambling eggs, scramble your words to make Humpty Dumpty words! Sometimes it is fun to mix up the letters in a word, then put them back together, just like in the nursery rhyme. Here's an example. Spelling word: **bake**. Scrambled: **keab**, **eakb** . . . finally . . . **bake** again. Hopefully, you will have more luck than all the king's men!

Words to Know

physical learner

A person who learns best while doing activities, such as a science experiment. This person is usually athletic and active. Games like charades help this person learn.

- Highlight the hard parts of the word you are studying. Maybe your word is **strong**, and you keep forgetting that **g** at the end. Get out that trusty highlighter and make those letters stand out. Try to decide why that part of the word is giving you a difficult time. Is there a rule that you can apply to it? Is it irregular? If no particular spelling rule sounds helpful, maybe highlighting your troublesome area and paying special attention to it will help you out!
- Make pyramid words. Practice writing them, deleting either the first or last letter each time you write the word. Take the word **pyramid** as an example.

pyramid
pyrami
ryami
yami
yam
am
a

Your turn. Make a pyramid out of the word **everything**. Now make one out of your last name. How about your first and last name? How many letters are in those words together? It could be a really big pyramid!

FOLLOW THE LINE

Another trick to remember how to spell is to outline the word with a shape. Can you see which word fits in which outline?

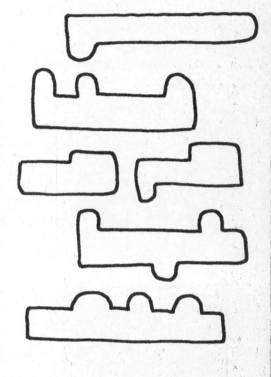

bicycle
milkshake
path milk
grammar
helmet

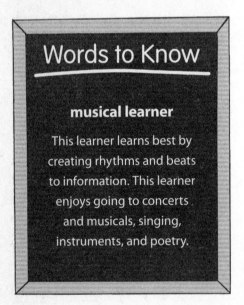

Words to Know

visual learner

Individuals who learn best through activities where they have to look at and analyze things. These learners love arts and crafts, making posters, and creating projects to demonstrate knowledge. Visual learners enjoy games like Pictionary.

Words to Know

musical learner

This learner learns best by creating rhythms and beats to information. This learner enjoys going to concerts and musicals, singing, instruments, and poetry.

- Use a tape recorder to practice spelling. Spell words aloud into a tape recorder and listen to your own voice as you practice writing the words. How do you sound? Like a pretty good teacher? If you enjoy spelling your words to a rhythm, you could spell your words out loud and then practice the spelling list that way.

- Use dry pasta, Alphabets cereal, alphabet soup, or even magnetic letters to spell. Were you able to find all the letters in the alphabet? Did you accidentally eat some of your words? Using your hands to form words can be a lot of fun. Using more than one of your five senses at a time can stimulate your memory and help you remember things longer.

- If you really want to get creative, how about writing your words in whipped cream? Practice writing the words on waxed paper, and then even have a couple of bites in order to help with the cleanup! Shaving cream also works well and is much easier to wipe up. However, it's definitely not as tasty.

- Cut out letters from magazines to write your spelling words. Glue the words onto a sheet of construction paper. When you are working on this project, use the big, colorful letters from advertisements. They're easier to work with because they are bigger than the small print in the newspaper or magazine articles. It's even fun to cut out photographs in magazines to illustrate your spelling words.

- Make a word search on graph paper. Write each of the words you are studying up and down, across, or diagonally in the squares. Next, fill in the empty squares with random letters. Wait a little bit, then give yourself a test. Can you find them all? More importantly, did you spell them all correctly?

Get a Study Buddy

Like a lot of things, studying spelling can be more fun with a partner. You could have a lot of fun writing words with shaving cream, sorting pasta, or making each other word searches. Don't worry if each of you likes different ways to learn to spell words. Those differences might even help you review words, and you can learn something new about a friend that maybe you didn't know before.

Obviously, there are lots of ways to practice spelling, and none of them have to be boring! As you progress in the book, you'll find a whole bunch more ideas. Chapter 9 is full of additional games and practice methods. Pick a few to try throughout the book. Don't worry if they don't all sound fun or helpful. If one strategy doesn't work for you, that's okay. Just give another one a try. Remember, everyone learns in his or her own way. There's not one way to study that is better than another.

Look, Cover, Write, Check

While there are clearly a whole lot of ways to study words, there is one system that seems foolproof. Look. Cover. Write. Check. Once you get in the habit of using this four-step process, you will have a good study strategy in your back pocket, no matter how difficult the word. You can also use this method to study other subjects besides spelling. It might come in handy for learning science facts or memorizing math formulas.

Try This

Egg Timer Time

Sometimes using a timer can really help you study. The timer watches the clock so you can focus on your words. Try an egg timer from the kitchen, or maybe there's a sports stopwatch around your house that you've used for swimming or track. Ask either your mom or dad for help if you're unsure how to use the timer.

Words to Know

visualization

The process of imagining or picturing something that is not in front of you, either by seeing it in your mind's eye or by remembering the item.

Look

This seems obvious, but here's what you do. Look at your spelling word. Say it out loud. *Really* look at it. Give that word at least ten seconds of your complete attention. Let's take a pretty tough word to use as our example: **furniture**. Write down **furniture** on a note card or piece of scratch paper and then say **furniture** out loud. Do you notice anything about this word that might help you remember how to spell it? Perhaps you noticed that it has three syllables. It can be divided into three sections: **fur•ni•ture**. The letter **u** appears twice, which is kind of unusual.

Take Cover!

The next step is to cover up the word. Right now, cover up **furniture**. Use an index card, a bookmark, or even your hand if you want. All you really need to do is cover the word up so you can't see it. Can you visualize, or imagine, what the word looks like? What does it start with? What letter does it end with? Do you remember anything else about the word? If you need to close your eyes to do that, then do so. If you can't see the word in your mind, go back to step one and look at the word again. Do this as many times as you need to. Concentrate on learning the word, not on how long it takes you. Remember, as you work on this process in the future, it will all get a lot easier.

Write On!

Fold your note card or piece of scratch paper in half. With the writing instrument of your choice, write out the word that you covered up.

Check It Out!

The last step involves checking out what you wrote and comparing it to the correct spelling. If you got the word right, good for you! You deserve an A+. If you messed up, don't worry. No one gets every word right on the first try. Take a break and try it again. Before you do, figure out what part of the word you had trouble with. Thinking about **furniture**, did you write an **a** instead of an **i**? Did you leave out an **r** or a **u**?

Using a Chart to Track Progress

Everyone likes to see that they are improving and to see how far they've progressed, whether it's counting how many sit-ups you can do, how many pounds you've lost, or how many inches taller you have grown. This is true in spelling as well. It helps to be able to see your success so you can celebrate your accomplishments. You also want to be able to quickly recognize areas with which you are having a tough time. Sometimes, being able to identify problems will make tackling them easier. For example, if you notice that when you study eight words you only get about four right, perhaps you should study fewer words at a time.

Think Positive

Read the following statements. Which seems like an easier problem to solve?

OFF TO SPELL

Can you figure out where Tony is going?

— — — — — — —

The first letter is in *past* but not *part*.

The second letter sounds like what you do with your eyes.

The third letter is the eighth letter of the alphabet.

The fourth letter is in *noon* and *moon* but not in *June*.

The fifth letter is the same as the one we just did.

The sixth letter is in the word *spell* two times.

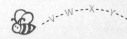

- I can't spell.
- I'm having trouble spelling words that have suffixes at the ending.

Here's another set of statements.

- I can't spell the continents.
- I can spell Europe and Asia, but I'm really having trouble with Australia.

Obviously, the second statement in each example seems better. Sometimes when we are having trouble with something, it's frustrating. That frustration makes us just want to stop doing the activity so we won't feel bad anymore. Maybe you felt this way when you tried something new in the past. Maybe it was learning to play soccer or baseball. Maybe it was cooking. To make things easier, identify what, exactly, is difficult for you. Then you will be able to develop some strategies to make things easier.

Measuring Progress

How do you want to keep track of your goals? Do you want to write everything in a notebook? Would you prefer to make a chart on a poster board? Maybe you and a parent want to set up a chart or spreadsheet on your computer. Find a method that works for you and that you will stick to. Next, decide what successes you'd like to keep track of. Is it A+ spelling tests in school? The number of words you've learned each week? Pick a goal that is reasonable for you but not so hard to achieve that it will make your head ache just thinking about it!

Start small. Instead of charting 100 percents on your spelling tests, maybe you could start with the goal of earning a B or an A. You could even make things a little bit easier than that.

MISTAKES TO A-V-O-I-D

It's All About What You *Can* Do!

No matter how frustrated you are, thinking negatively won't help. Instead, be positive! With practice, you can spell just about any word. It just takes time and practice. Instead of saying, "I can't spell," or even, "I can't spell words with confusing suffixes," turn things around. Try saying, "I know how to spell some easy words," and "I'm going to work on the suffixes 'ness' and 'ment' this week."

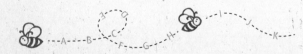

For example, if you've failed the last three out of five spelling tests, aim to pass the next three out of five. Here's another example: If learning twenty words a week is hard for you, try keeping track of how many words you do get right each week. No matter what, don't set yourself up to fail! No marathon runner starts an exercise program with the intention of winning the Boston Marathon—most just want to finish it! If you interviewed marathon runners or Olympians, those athletes would tell you that they set multiple goals over time. If they can do that, so can you!

Chart Making 101

After you know what you want to chart and what you hope to accomplish, it's time to make that chart! If you are computer-minded, make a super spreadsheet on the computer. If you're the type of person who likes to be able to look at your chart often, get out the pencil, ruler, and markers and design a grid on a poster board. Then you can thumbtack it to a wall in your room to keep track of your progress often. Some people like making a chart in the first page of their spelling notebook; that way, it's all in one place. No matter what you decide, vow to take some time to work on these goals. So . . . get ready, get set, and make that goal!

Try This

Everyone likes prizes. Once you've decided on your goals, make up some prizes. Maybe you like gold star stickers. For larger goals, you could plan to go out for ice cream. You get the idea—plan to give yourself a little reward to make meeting your goal a little more special.

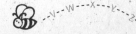

Just the Facts, Ma'am

Basic Rules

In this chapter, we're going to review some of the most basic rules. You can't avoid it. There are a number of basic rules that really do help you learn how to spell. Once you have mastered them, these rules will help you learn to spell a great majority of words correctly. Though many people will admit the wide variety of words in the English language can be a challenge to spell correctly, most will agree that a large number of words are obedient. In other words, they like to follow the rules! So, put these next few rules to memory and be prepared to find success. Do you know any of the rules already?

A Quick Rule

Let's start with one of the easiest rules to remember. When you spell words that have a **q** in them, always follow that **q** with a **u**. Some examples are **queen** and **quiet**. Two other words are **quiz** and **quaint**. There are only a few times when

Spelling Rules

1. "u" follows "q" in words like "queen"

Just the Facts, Ma'am

following a **q** with a **u** isn't the right thing to do, and that's when the word ends in a **q**, like **Iraq**. Boy, things would sure be simple if every spelling rule was so easy to learn.

Check for Vowels

Another rule that's easy to remember is the Vowel Rule. That is, each syllable in a word must have a vowel in it. Here are three examples:

Colorado	Col•o•rad•o
Mississippi	Mis•sis•sip•pi
elephant	el•e•phant

Each syllable in these rather long words has a vowel in it. Even short words follow this example, such as the word **able**. Able is two syllables, **a•ble**. Notice that even the second syllable has a vowel, even though it is the sneaky silent **e**. If you have a syllable in a word without a vowel, it is probably misspelled.

Studying three-syllable words is good practice not only with spelling, but with listening for vowel and consonant sounds. Here are sixteen three-syllable words you might want to add to your ongoing spelling list. Some of these words, such as **dinosaur**, would be perfect to illustrate. Pick four of the words and draw a picture to help you remember the word.

exercise	favorite	electric	terrible
dangerous	dinosaur	amazement	horizon
continent	family	library	period
newspaper	credible	dynamite	transition

Words to Know

syllable

Words are divided into syllables. Say a word out loud, and clap its beats. **Good** has one beat, or one syllable. **Afternoon** has three syllables, so it is divided as: **af•ter•noon**. You can also divide a word between the two middle consonants. The word **dinner** is divided in between the two n's: **din•ner**. Again, notice how each beat of the word has a vowel. If you're not sure where to divide a word, the dictionary is the perfect tool to help you!

vowel

There are five vowels: **a, e, i, o,** and **u**. In addition, **y** is sometimes considered a vowel, like in **by** or **hardy**. Each word needs a vowel in order to be called a word. One popular word, **I** is made up of only one vowel!

  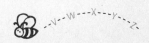

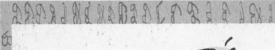

GOODBYE, EEE!

Here's a rhyme to remember when you are adding -ing to a word.

WHEN -ING COMES TO STAY, LITTLE e RUNS AWAY!

For example, *frame* turns into *framing*. Can you think of more words where the e disappears when -ing is added?

The C Rule

Here's another rule that's pretty easy to remember. When you have a word that ends in **c**, such as **picnic** or **traffic**, you have to add a **k** before adding **-ing** or **-y** to the word.

- Picnic becomes picnicking. We are going on a **picnic** in March. We enjoy **picnicking** in the mountains.
- Panic becomes panicking or panicky. I start to **panic** if I'm going to be late. Sometimes, my **panicking** makes me forget things and then I'm even later! My family tells me not to be so **panicky**.
- Traffic becomes trafficking. The policeman had to help guide **traffic** in the snow and rain. He was also watching for people who were **trafficking**, or transferring, fruits and vegetables across the state border.

Superhero Letters

These rules have to do with vowels. The five letters **a, e, i, o,** and **u** can have so many sounds, they really should be called superhero letters because they're able to transform their sounds as they need to. I imagine poor letters like **k** or **b** can be jealous at times because they can only make one specific sound! For our spelling purposes, we need to remember that for the most part, there are **two kinds of vowel sounds, long and short**.

Just the Facts, Ma'am

The Long and Short of It

Let's start with the easiest sound a vowel can make—the looonnnnggggg sound. In a long vowel, we hear the sound of the letter, just like when you recite it when you say the alphabet out loud. For example, **ice** has the long **i** sound. You actually hear the letter **i** when you say the word. You also hear that long **i** in the words **item**, **mice**, **idea**, and **mighty**.

Let's look at examples with the letter **a**. You hear the long **a** in the words **cake**, **ache**, **rake**, **fake**, **and bake**. You can hear the **e** in **feed** and **need**, and the long **o** sound in **open**, **cope**, **hope**, **and elope**. If you're not sure how to pronounce a vowel, you can look at the pronunciation key, which is right next to each word in the dictionary. A long vowel sound will have a line over the vowel, like this: ‾.

Try This

Rhyming Words

Many times, words that rhyme are spelled alike. Let's use the word **ate** as our example. How many words can you think of that rhyme with **ate**? Go through the alphabet and try on letters—**crate**, **date**, **fate**, **gate**. How many words can you discover that have that same long **a** sound, followed by **te**?

The Long U

Can you think of any words that have a long **u** sound? Here's one to get you started: unique. (notice the second **u** following that **q**!) Okay, your turn. Can you think of any other words with long **u** sounds?

 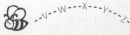

Try This

Short Vowel Sounds

These five phrases might be helpful to you when you are looking for easy, identifiable short vowel sounds: **A as in apple, E as in egg, I as in insect, O as in orange, and U as in umbrella**. Can you make up your own phrases for the short vowels? Maybe you'd like all of your phrases to have to do with animals.

Short Vowel Activity

Here's another activity to work on rhyming short vowel sounds. Write down the letters **ba**. If you add a consonant after, you can make a variety of words that have a short **a** sound, such as **bad** or **bag**. How many different words can you make by adding just one or two consonants to **ba**? Try for fifteen.

Short But Not Tiny

The short vowel sounds in words are more difficult to hear. Some teachers say the short vowel sounds are soft. While some students have no trouble hearing a short vowel, others find it most useful to study words that have the same short vowel sound and learn that way. Which way is easiest for you? Here are words with a short **a** sound: **mask**, **task**, **act**, and **bag**. Words that have a short **i** include: **list**, **wish**, and **is**. Can you tell the difference between the short and long vowel sounds? If so, you'll be able to spell the words by hearing them.

Spelling students who don't learn best by listening to the sounds of the letters might get the short vowel sounds confused. Some of them are hard to hear, especially if you aren't used to listening for them. Once again, you can go back to the good old dictionary and look at the pronunciation key for help. A short vowel sound will be have a curved line over it, like this: ˘. The curved line looks like a parenthesis on its side. Usually, practicing words and listening for similar sounds, especially rhyming sounds, can be very helpful when you are learning to spell.

Rhyming Words

If you are determined to create a list of words that have a short **a** sound, try rhyming. For example, words that have the same short **a** sound as **map** are **trap**, **slap**, **cap**, and **tap**. If you can hear that 'ap' sound, you can easily pick up the spellings of a whole bunch of other words. Once you have mastered those words, you can add some words with other syllables, such as **happy** or **tapping**. Then, it's just a matter of course to learn to spell more difficult words that have that 'ap' sound, such as **trapeze**, **apple**, or **happiness**.

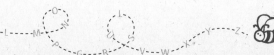

WISE AS AN OWL

This owl is giving a lesson to her students. Can you spot the nine words spelled wrong here?

GREATFUL
WINDOW
FOURTY
PILLOW
SCRAMBLE
CAREFUL
DECIEVE
BELEIVE
WEDNESDAY

FUNGIS
PENGIUN
MAGIC
ROOMATE
DEFENITE
EGGPLANT
UMBRELLA
SLOWLIE

SILENT LETTERS

In English, all the letters in the alphabet (except J, O, V, and Y) can be silent.

Spelling errors are all around us. Next time you go out, see if you can spot any in shop windows or advertisements.

I Before E Except After C

Have you heard of that well-known spelling rule yet? When spelling words that have an **ie** combination, always position the **i** before the **e**—unless, of course, the letters **i** and **e** come after a **c**. This might be the most famous spelling rule ever because it's so easy to remember and because it really does work! Words that have the combination of letters **i** and **e** together usually do go in that order. Here are some examples: **tie**, **thief**, **brief**, and **shriek**.

Exceptions, Exceptions

Not every word wants to follow the rules. The **i** before **e** rule works most of the time—but not all the time. There are several words that do not contain the letter **c** but do have an **e** that comes before an **i**. Here are two crazy sayings that pretty much incorporate all the words that have **e** before **i**.

- Neither leisured foreigner seized the weird height.
- Eight counterfeit steins deceived the deity.

Whew! Some of those words are pretty fancy and might be unfamiliar to you. You almost need to get out the dictionary just to understand the exceptions!

Vowel and Consonant Combinations

There are two vowel and consonant combinations that are fairly common. These patterns are so popular that they've been given labels. They are usually known as VCCV or VCCCV combinations. The Vs and Cs stand for vowels and consonants. Let's take a closer look at each.

Try This

I Before E Revisited

You know the famous spelling rule: **i** before **e** except after **c**. It's catchy, but there's a little more to it. When **e** and **i** combine to make the sound **ay** as in **neighbor** and **weigh**, the **e** comes before the **i**. Can you think of four exceptional words to add to neighbor and weigh?

Just the Facts, Ma'am

VCCV

These words have two consonants sandwiched by two vowels. Sometimes the consonants are doubled, such as in **attack**. Other times, there are consonant combinations. Here are twenty words of varying levels of difficulty:

attack	effect	effort	pillow
tunnel	college	fellow	challenge
cassette	buffalo	entire	service
chimney	orbit	thunder	suspend
ignite	compare	blanket	pretzel

The Dreaded VCCCCV

VCCCCV. Expand your brain! Can you think of any words that might fit this pattern? Here's one—instruct. N, S, T, and R are all consonants that are surrounded by vowels. Can you think of any others?

VCCCV

Believe it or not, there are a whole lot of words that have three consonants together in the middle of a word! Sometimes, the word is divided into syllables in the middle of these

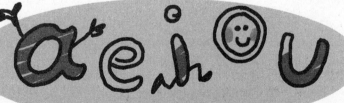

THE LONG WAY

There are four words for each vowel. Only one of them in each pair is pronounced with a long vowel sound. Can you tell which it is?

FUNNY PURE   ROW LOST

TREE PET

NOW ROPE

HILL RIGHT

GRAPE RATTLE

RULER SUN

GREEN LEFT

BIKE LIFT   PAST TRADE

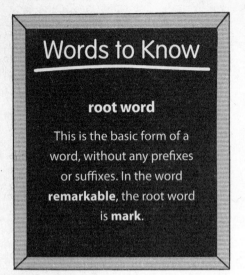

Words to Know

root word

This is the basic form of a word, without any prefixes or suffixes. In the word **remarkable**, the root word is **mark**.

Try This

Radical Changes

Prefixes can completely change the meaning of a root word. When you add prefixes like **re** and **dis** to a root word like **appear**, you get words that mean totally different things. Can you draw a picture to illustrate these two meanings? Can you think of any other prefixes that can change the meaning of a root word like that?

consonants. Other times, the three letters combine to make one sound, such as **str** in the word **distract**. Here are twenty-four words that fit this pattern:

Christmas	Congress	English	although
complaint	complex	conflict	construction
contract	contrast	distrust	exchange
luncheon	pumpkin	subtract	transform
extra	improve	instead	contraction
castle	mishandle	bramble	puzzle

Prefixes

Prefixes are short groups of letters that are added to the beginning of a root word to change its meaning. One common prefix is **re**, which means **again**. If you **retake** a test, you are taking the test again. Another common prefix is **mis**, which means **wrong or not right**. If someone **mislabeled** the cans in your kitchen, you might open a can of nasty asparagus tips instead of, say, crunchy corn. You get the picture—the cans were labeled wrong. Other words that have the **mis** prefix are **misuse** and **mistake**.

Learn and Use!

If you know some basic prefixes, you will be able to spell the beginning of a great variety of words. Here are six common prefixes that are used in hundreds of words. The meanings of the prefixes are also included, as well as examples to show how a prefix can completely change the meaning of a word.

Prefixes

PREFIX (MEANING)	ROOT WORD	COMBINED WORD
dis (not)	appear	disappear
un (not)	tie	untie
mis (not right)	take	mistake
re (do again)	turn	return
de (from)	tail	detail
ex (out of or from)	tract	extract

Suffixes

Suffixes are groups of letters that are added to the ending of words. Just like a prefix, these letters can change the meaning of a word.

Suffixes

SUFFIX (MEANING)	ROOT WORD	COMBINED WORD
ful (full of)	care	careful
ness (a condition of)	bitter, happy	bitterness, happiness
less (without)	penny, care	penniless, careless
y (characterized by)	cloud	cloudy
en (caused to be)	bright	brighten
able (able to)	wash	washable

PREFIX THIS

This alien is learning English. He's discovering what a big difference it makes if you put some new letters in front of a word. Can you help him with these?

If someone is not polite they are
A: unpolite
B: impolite
C: apolite

If you take paper off a gift you:
A: dewrap
B: rewrap
C: unwrap

If you redraw something you:
A: draw it the first time
B: erase it
C: draw it again

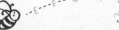 

Headline Headache

Not a Real Word

Many employers shake their heads when they get resumes with misspelled words. Someone probably got a laugh when they read this: "I am uncareful of plants and animals." Hmmmm . . . the prefix **un** means **not**. The suffix **ful** means **full of**. So the person was "not full of care" for plants and animals? Do you think this person got the job?

When a Root Word Ends in a Vowel

There's an important rule to remember when you want to add suffixes to words. Sometimes it is necessary to change the spelling of a word in order to add the suffix. If a word has a silent **e** at the end, such as in the words **have** or **like**, you drop that **e** when you add a suffix if the suffix begins with a vowel. For example, you might **have** the flu. John might not ever remember **having** the flu. Here, that **e** after the **v** was dropped when you added **ing**. This pattern can be used with words such as **save**, which becomes **saving**, and **drive**, which becomes **driving**.

When a Root Word Ends in a Consonant

When you are adding a suffix that begins with a consonant to a word that already ends in a consonant, you can keep all the letters in a word. For instance, **slow** becomes **slowly**. **Careful** becomes **carefully**.

Highlight Those Headaches!

Remembering all of these rules and all of the crazy exceptions takes time. As you read further into the book, you will also realize that there are a lot of exceptions to all kinds of rules. Finally, sometimes some parts of the words will be harder to spell than others. Have you noticed any rules that are hard for you to remember? For many people, it is figuring out how to spell words with suffixes. To make things easier for you, write down or highlight the words that give you trouble all the time. Once you see the same word or vowel combination over and over again, you'll start to learn it.

Just the Facts, Ma'am

Admit, Then Move On

A spelling obstacle that really stumps a lot of people is hearing the short vowels. No matter how hard they try, some people can never hear the difference between a short **o** and a short **a** sound. If you have this problem, always double-check the middle letters of short words when you spell them.

Other people have a difficult time with vowel combinations, such as **ae** or **ia**. Don't be afraid to admit that you need to double-check certain words. When you come across a word you're not sure of, go back to the strategy we covered in Chapter 1: Look, Cover, Write, Check.

Slow and Sure

Once you've identified which types of words you always have a tough time spelling, give yourself some time to practice and study them. Perhaps at your school you have a new spelling list each week. For some students, this is no problem. But for other kids, it can be very difficult to learn words so quickly. The beauty of this book is that you don't have to go that quickly! Perhaps you will need to spend a long time working on the types of words in this chapter. There's nothing wrong with that. Feel free to go back to Chapter 1 and use some of the spelling activities. Chapter 8 also has some suggestions for studying and for making studying fun. Good luck!

Study with Scrabble

Put that Scrabble game to good use by using it to help you learn prefixes and suffixes. First, spell out a simple word, such as **test**. Now see if you can add any suffixes or prefixes to the word. Maybe you added **re** or **pre** to make **retest** or **pretest**. You could also add **ed** or **ing**. If you want a real challenge, see if you can add both a prefix and a suffix to the word, such as **pretesting**. See how many points you can add up.

Chapter 3

These Words Aren't Like the Others

Irregular Nouns

Nouns are people, places, and things. There are all different kinds of nouns. Some name general items like dogs. Others name specific people, places, or things. Some nouns describe ideas or ownership. And some nouns are rebels! They just don't have any need to fit in, spelling-wise. From now on, refer to them as irregular nouns. Their spelling is out of sorts, and their patterns don't fit too many of the basic rules in Chapter 2. Though these crazy words can be frustrating to spell, you need to accept these oddball words and try and learn how to spell them.

Good News!

After careful research, it's been discovered that the spelling of all these irregular words is not quite as strange or difficult as first thought. Some of the words can even be grouped together to make better sense of them and see their patterns. With that in mind, let's get started. It's time to be a detective and examine these words closely.

Try This

Think Positively!

These crazy words will not get the best of you! You will certainly find a way to overcome the most difficult spellings. Keep that in mind and get ready to dive in.

A noun is a person. place. or thing.

VARIOUS VERBS

Most of these verbs are irregular, but four have snuck in that don't belong. Can you tell which ones they are?

begun

break

grew

shake

swam

won

spent

met

put

split

spread

bid

SIT OR SET

Sometimes it can be confusing when to use certain verbs. **Sit** means "to rest or occupy a seat." **Set** means "to put or lay" something. Sit in a chair and set the book down.

MISTAKES TO A-V-O-I-D

Tricky Collective Nouns

Be careful! Some nouns start out plural. They are called collective nouns, and they name a group of things or people. Some examples of collective nouns are **staff**, **group**, **department**, and **jury**. Because these words describe more than one thing already, you don't ever change their forms. The **staff** might **gather** in the library, or the **jury** might **listen** to a case. Under the right circumstances, these nouns can be plural. For example, there might be **two juries** in the courthouse listening to cases.

Oddball Nouns

Some forms of plural nouns are so peculiar, they get a chapter of their own. Chapter 6 tells you everything you need to know about spelling these special nouns, whether there are one or 100 of them! If you're curious about them, in a nutshell, these nouns completely change forms, like **louse** and **lice**.

Always the Same

Some nouns never change forms. They like staying the same, no matter what. One example of this type of noun is the word **deer**. **Deer** stays **deer**, whether you have one or a whole herd roaming around your backyard. Finally, some words change spelling, but only the middle vowels are different. For example, **foot** becomes **feet** and one **tooth** becomes many **teeth**.

Irregular Verbs

Most people are familiar with action verbs, which are words that show action. The words **walk**, **run**, and **swim** are all examples of action verbs. Most of the time, when you need to change a verb from one tense to another, you simply add the letters 'ed' or 'ing.' Here are some examples: **started**, **walked**, **fished**, **hearing**, **speaking**, **bowling**, and **talked**. However, there are quite a few irregular verbs that don't follow this pattern. Sometimes the end of the word changes when an ending is added. Other times, the whole word changes.

Many people feel that memorizing all of the different rules for the exceptions can be difficult. In fact, some people can get easily frustrated, because they focus on sets of rules instead of proper forms of irregular verbs. In this case, it's just necessary to learn the various forms of these strange verbs. When you come across the strange verbs, you must simply memorize the

These Words Aren't Like the Others

proper tenses. Get ready to Look, Cover, Write, and Check for a while. Good luck!

One More Thing

A lot of the following verbs might be familiar to you. You might already use the correct forms of the verbs in your regular conversations. Put that knowledge to good use! If you already know that a boy or a girl would **swim** in the pool today but **swam** yesterday, then concentrate on spelling swim and swam instead of trying to remember what irregular list **swim** is on. Once again, rules are great, but sometimes they just get in the way of learning.

Present and Past Tense Only

Here is a list of irregular verbs. If you know your grammar, you know that there are three basic tenses of verbs—present, past, and future. Because this book is focused on spelling and not grammar, we're only going to focus on the present and past tense of twenty verbs. How many of these are you familiar with?

PRESENT	PAST	PRESENT	PAST
become	became	keep	kept
bite	bit	make	made
build	built	pay	paid
catch	caught	ride	rode
dig	dug	run	ran
drive	drove	sell	sold
eat	ate	stick	stuck
feed	fed	wake	woke
get	got	write	wrote
go	went		

Headline Headache

See-Saw

Here's an actual quotation from a college student's term paper: "I saw Jane here but she didn't saw me." Oops! Looks like the author used the wrong form of **saw**. Now it sounds like Jane could be very dangerous! Let's keep Jane away from all of her father's tools.

MISTAKES TO A-V-O-I-D

Breath or Breathe?

Let's look at the words **breath** and **breathe**. Do you know which is which? These are commonly mistaken for each other! The only thing that makes them different from each other is that silent **e**, but it sure makes a difference in how you use and say the word out loud! Let's make things simple. **Breath** is a noun. The doctor might ask you to take a **breath**. **Breathe** is a verb. A man might **breathe** deeply while sleeping.

Which of these words do you already know? Do you use any of these words often when you talk to your family and friends? Go ahead and mark these words with a green highlighter or put a star or checkmark next to them. You are already a spelling wizard! Remember, just knowing the correct forms of irregular verbs is a big success.

V.I.V.—Very Irregular Verb!

Did you only count nineteen verbs in the list? That's because there's one very important verb left that is so special it needs a section all its own. Drum roll, please. I'd like to introduce to you . . . the magical verb . . . **be**! The verb **be** refers to a state of **being**. If that's not confusing enough, the forms of this **be** verb can also be called a linking verb, because grammarians like to say the linking verb links the subject of a sentence to the predicate. The predicate is the part of the sentence that tells what the subject is doing—or being! The girl

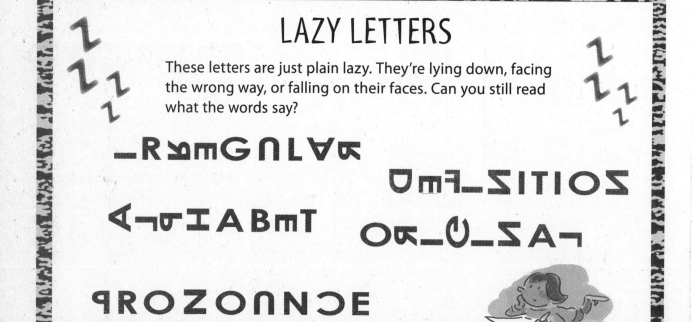

LAZY LETTERS

These letters are just plain lazy. They're lying down, facing the wrong way, or falling on their faces. Can you still read what the words say?

IRREGULAR

OPPOSITION

VOCHABET

OPPOSITE

PROZOUNCE

These Words Aren't Like the Others

was hungry. The boy **is talking to his friend**. There are five main linking verbs, which are all forms of the extremely odd-ball verb **be**. They are **am**, **is**, **are**, **was**, and **were**. These linking verbs are very common. You can find them in just about any newspaper article, magazine, or novel. Lucky for you, they are also easy to spell.

Time to Practice

Now that you are familiar with the **be** words, it's time to put them to good use. Use the forms of **be** to fill in the following blanks:

Jane _____ ten today. She _____ nine just yesterday.

I _____ older than Jane. In fact, both my brother and I _____ a lot older than Jane!

We _____ going to see Jane today, but she went to a party without us.

Words from Other Countries

America really is a melting pot. The United States is filled with people who either came from other countries or are descended from people who did. Because of this, the English language is a mixture of words from all sorts of backgrounds and cultures. This makes the English language special. But all these different backgrounds and cultures also make it difficult to learn to spell a great variety of words in the English language. The rest of this chapter will focus on Latin, French, and Spanish because many English words were originally words in one of these three languages.

It's Irregular

The most important irregular verbs are the forms of **be** (am, is, are, was, were), the forms of **have** (have, having, has, had), and **do** (do, doing, did).

Words to Know

action verb

Action verbs are verbs that show movement of some kind. **Walk, write, eat, blink,** and **smile** are all action verbs. Can you think of any sneaky action verbs that show action but maybe aren't very noticeable? How about **think**? Try to name ten action verbs that you can do in school. Are any of them sneaky?

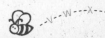

37

Words in the Kitchen

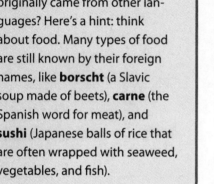

Can you think of any words that originally came from other languages? Here's a hint: think about food. Many types of food are still known by their foreign names, like **borscht** (a Slavic soup made of beets), **carne** (the Spanish word for meat), and **sushi** (Japanese balls of rice that are often wrapped with seaweed, vegetables, and fish).

Back from the Dead

See if you can find another dead language. And here's a bonus point—see if there are any words in that language that we use in today's speech.

However, there are many other languages that have left their mark on English. Have you ever heard of **karate** or **manga**? Both are Japanese words that are commonly used in English today. Karate is a form of self-defense, and manga are a type of comics. Has anyone ever said "**Gesundheit!**" to you after you sneezed? That's a German wish for good health. Have you ever heard someone describe something that's not real as **phony**? That comes from the Irish word for ring. Merchants used to sell rings that were not worth as much as they sold them for. People started using the word for ring to describe anything that was fake.

Latin Origins

First, Latin is a dead language. That means no one currently uses it to speak. But when people did speak Latin, it was way back when the Romans ruled a lot of the world. The Roman Empire originated in Italy but spread to a lot of places. They went to the continent of Africa, Spain, France, and even as far north as England.

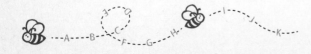 

When in Rome

Much of the English language has Latin origins. Some scholars say half of all English words came from Latin words. Do you feel smarter yet? You've been speaking another language and didn't even know it! The reason you want to examine the roots of some words is because some of these words will appear time and again in spelling lists, vocabulary lists, and finally, in history and science areas. If you can identify them and have a better idea of their origin, it might make it easier for you to spell and define similar words. There are three main tricks that might help you figure out if a word came from Latin.

- Long **e** and **i**: The words **magi, cacti**, and **alumni** come directly to the English language from Latin. Each word ends in an **i** with a long **i** sound. Some words with a long **e** sound are **veto**, **senior**, and **medium**.
- Letter **c** sounds like **k**: The following words are derived from Latin and have the letter **c** in them, but have a hard **k** sound: **college**, **constitution**, and **locale**.
- Don't forget **gn**: A letter combination that is unique to Latin words is **gn**. In words that come from Latin, it makes an **n** sound but is spelled with a **gn**. Two examples are **design** and **assign**.

LATIN SCRAMBLE

Somebody has mixed up these letters. Can you put them back together and match them with their proper definition?*

soecitdm   to pass over or across

teicadt   to read aloud

tarsitn   not from here

ciciafp   found at home

nilae   the largest ocean

*All of these words come originally from Latin.

English speakers know words from at least 100 different languages. These include words like sushi, karaoke, and karate from Japanese and déjà vu, bon voyage, and hors d'oeuvres from French. Can you think of others?

 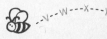

The Last Letter

The letter **z** is rare in words of Latin origin. Therefore, any word that has a **z** in it probably comes from a language other than Latin. Feel like doing a little bit of research? Look up the word **maze**. Where does this word come from? Can you use it in a sentence? Can you name two words **maze** rhymes with?

Romans in Britain

Did you know that the reason so many words in the English language are Latin in origin is because the early Romans lived in England? For at least 400 years during the height of the Roman Empire, the Romans lived in the area now known as Britain. During this time, the Britons adopted many Latin words and began using them in their daily language.

Latin Suffixes and Prefixes

We've already discussed suffixes and prefixes a bit in Chapter 2, but did you know that many common suffixes and prefixes are of Latin origin? They all have interesting meanings. When you know how they are spelled and what they mean, this knowledge can help you spell and define words you don't know. Here are twenty common prefixes and suffixes from Latin.

PREFIX	MEANING	EXAMPLE
di-	to divide	We're going to dissect a frog in science class.
ante-	before	Antebellum houses are in beautiful Georgia.
pre-	before	We went to a movie preview.
dis-	apart or away	The room was in complete disarray.
inter-	between	Watch for heavy traffic on the interchange.
sub-	under	The submarine was painted silver.
re-	again	The students moaned when they had to retake a test.
bi-	two	My bicycle tire needed to be pumped up.
quad-	four	That quadruped had four legs and was really fast.
bio-	life	In high school, you might take biology.
ex-	out	We painted the exterior of the house.
tele-	distance	He made a telephone call to Greece.

SUFFIX	MEANING	EXAMPLE
-ist	one who	A scientist is one who studies science.
-able	capable of being	That car is drivable.
-ic	having the nature of	I would not want to arm-wrestle the bionic superhero!

These Words Aren't Like the Others

Spanish Words

There are also a lot of words in the English language that come from Spanish. Some people guess that there might be as many as 10,000! Many words that have a double 'L' in their spelling are Spanish. Some examples are **alligator**, **vanilla**, **chinchilla**, and **armadillo**. Those two 'Ls' together make kind of a y sound.

Definitions, Please

Some Spanish words have interesting origins. For example, the word **cargo** means 'to load' in Spanish. **Alligator** means 'the lizard.' **Ranch** comes from the Spanish word *rancho*. Other Spanish-origin words are **pronto**, **manatee**, **rodeo**, and **plaza**. We also get two weather-related words from the Spanish. Both **hurricane** and **tornado** are Spanish in origin. You might know more Spanish words than you think if you enjoy Mexican food. **Tacos**, **enchiladas**, and **burritos** are obviously Spanish words.

Creating More Words

Because America is a land of many languages and different cultures, new words are constantly being added to the English language. Each year, *Webster's Dictionary* adds a few words to its newest edition. The next time you look up a word in the dictionary, take some time to see what country the word originated from. Who knows? You might be speaking in far more languages than you ever imagined!

> ## Words to Know
>
> ### armadillo
>
> The **armadillo** is a cat-sized little mammal that looks like it is covered in armor. In fact, armadillo means 'the little armed one' in Spanish! Armadillos like to eat insects and are usually very shy. They also happen to be the state mammal of Texas.

> ### Try This
>
> ## New Words
>
> One of the newest words to enter the English vocabulary is **ginormous.** It's a combination of **gigantic** and **enormous**. What do you think of this word? Have you used it yet? Some words enter our language and then leave it again. One example of such a word might be **groovy.** What do you think about **ginormous**? Do you think it will stay in our everyday speech or will it be forgotten?

FROM THE SPANISH

English is mostly made up of two languages—French and German. But there are a lot of words from other languages as well. Here are some words borrowed from Spanish. Can you match them up with their original meaning?

alligator

thunderstorm

little donkey

ranch

little armored one

little pod

lizard

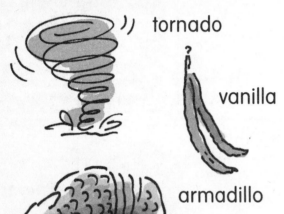

tornado

vanilla

armadillo

rancho

burrito

HALF AND HALF

Fifty words account for half of all the words we use in daily conversation. They are all one-syllable words like 'the,' 'have,' and 'you.' What other words do you use the most?

These Words Aren't Like the Others

French Words

Without the French, we wouldn't have the game show *Who Wants to Be a Millionaire?* Those very rich sounding words—**millionaire** and **billionaire**—come from the French. Here are a few words and their commonalities.

To 'aire' Is French

Both **billionaire** and **millionaire** are French. So is that card game, **solitaire**. The common letters in all of these are, of course, **aire**.

Sounds Like the Long A

When you see a word that ends with the letters **et** but sounds like a long **a**, it is most likely a French word. Some examples are **crochet**, **bouquet**, **ballet**, **buffet**, and **croquet**.

Try This

French Fun

Do you know what the French word **croquet** means? It's a fun game you can play outdoors. Do a little investigation about this sport, and perhaps you can even convince your family to play a game—all to help out your spelling, of course!

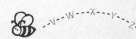

Chapter 4

Punctuation Rules

Words to Know

apostrophe

The apostrophe is the punctuation mark placed in between letters in a word to indicate that letters are missing or that a word is possessive. The words **don't** and **grandma's** both use this tiny but important notation.

Possessive Nouns

You wouldn't think so, but punctuation can often play a part in spelling a word correctly. You not only need to know where to put the correct letters, but you must also know whether the word needs a hyphen, space, or apostrophe. The reason there's a whole chapter on these things is that they fool and confuse a lot of people! If remembering what words need hyphens or apostrophes feels too overwhelming, just concentrate on a small number of specific words to master.

Showing Ownership

Possessive nouns are nouns that show possession or ownership. For most words, all you have to do is add **'s** to a word.

NOUN	POSSESSIVE STATEMENT	MEANING
student	student's pencil	the pencil that belongs to the student
boy	boy's DVD	the DVD that belongs to the boy
girl	girl's arm	the arm of the girl
house	house's windows	the windows in the house
mother	mother's kisses	the kisses the mother gave
doctor	doctor's answer	the answer the doctor gave

In each of these examples, can you pick out how the **'s** shows possession? The pencil and the DVD are both objects that you can actually pick up and hold. It is easy to see how these can belong to the student and the boy. In the next example, the arm is part of the girl's body. It isn't an object you can possess like a pencil or a DVD, but your arm definitely belongs to you. In the same way, the windows are a part of the house.

The last two examples—the mother's kisses and the doctor's answer—are a little more difficult to see. Kisses and answers aren't things you can see or hold, but the **'s** at the end of the word shows where they are coming from. The kisses come from the mother and the answer comes from the doctor.

See if you can turn these long phrases into short possessive phrases.

the feet of the baby _____

the shoes that belong to the boy _____

the building that belongs to the city _____

the program at the school _____

the largest race in Missouri _____

Is It Singular or Plural?

All of the words we've looked at so far have been singular nouns. This means there is only one of them. When there is more than one of an object, it is called a plural noun. Usually, all you do to turn a singular noun into a plural noun is add an **s** to the end of the word. Chapter 6 will go over all of the different ways to make a plural noun, but here are a few examples so we can talk about how to make a plural noun possessive.

 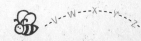

Try This

Don't Change the Meaning!

Using the wrong punctuation mark will change the meaning of the word, or even the meaning of a phrase or sentence. See if you can spot the difference between these two sentences: My beagle's stomach is in trouble. My beagles' stomach is in trouble. Now explain why one of the sentences is wrong.

The first sentence is correct. "My beagle's stomach" means the stomach of one beagle. But when you put the apostrophe after the **s**, as in "my beagles' stomach," that means you're talking about the stomach of more than one beagle. What a mess! How can two beagles share a stomach?

SINGULAR NOUN	PLURAL NOUN
animal	animals
snowflake	snowflakes
fish	fish
mouse	mice
child	children

What happens if you want to make a plural possessive noun? For example, let's say you are talking about food for two animals. The apostrophe goes after the **s** in **animals** like this: **the animals' food**. Here are some other examples using plural nouns:

PLURAL NOUN	POSSESSIVE PHRASE	EXAMPLE
boys	boys' lizards	The boys' lizards got loose in the dining room.
oceans	oceans' creatures	The oceans' creatures are all different colors.

Possessives, Not Plurals

A lot of people confuse possessives with regular plural nouns and either give them an apostrophe or forget them completely. Sometimes people aren't sure whether they are referring to a plural noun or a possessive noun.

All stuffed animal's are on sale today.

Yikes! Do you know what the mistake is? Seeing spelling mistakes like that can drive you crazy. Here, **animal's** is spelled wrong. The writer was simply referring to more than

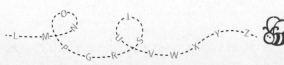

one animal, not that those animals own anything! The advertisement should read:

All stuffed animals are on sale today.

Pronouns and Possessives

Deciding what to do with a possessive pronoun is a difficult task. Basically, a possessive pronoun is the counterpart to a possessive noun. It shows ownership. In novels, you see pronouns a lot. And it makes sense—you would not want the writer to continually use a character's name.

Here's an example of when an author really should have used more pronouns: "Andrew went to the store. Andrew bought a gallon of milk. Andrew carried the milk home." Boy, reading that would get old fast! Instead, you might want to say, "Andrew went to the store. He bought a gallon of milk.

MISTAKES TO A-V-O-I-D

Plural to Possessive

When you come into contact with a noun that does not change forms when plural, such as **fish** or **deer**, simply add an apostrophe **s**. Example: **The fish's food**. Don't try anything crazy like the **fishes'** or **fishs'** food.

MINE AND YOURS

Which of these sentences has possessive nouns?

- [ ] That boy's skateboard is green.

- [ ] The dogs are running up the hill.

- [ ] My mother's apron is missing.

- [ ] The teams are going to play hockey.

- [ ] The cat's tail is twitching.

- [ ] The girl's journal is full of writing.

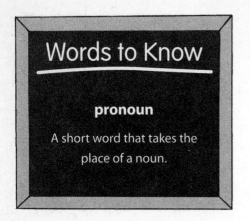

Words to Know

pronoun

A short word that takes the place of a noun.

Try This
It's Your Turn!

Write a sentence with a possessive pronoun for each of the following items in a garage:

* bike
* car
* skateboard

Here's an example: His bike is red.

He carried it home." As you can see, these sentences meant the same thing as the first example, but it sounds better.

The most common pronouns are:

I	me
he	him
she	her
they	them
we	us
it	you

Here are the most common possessive pronouns:

PRONOUN	POSSESSIVE PRONOUNS
I, me	my, mine
you	your
he	his
she	her, hers
they	their, theirs
we	our
it	its

Did you notice one thing in common about all of the pronouns listed? Not one of them has an apostrophe. This is important to note. Possessive pronouns never have an apostrophe. The words themselves change. Because you are not adding anything (like **'s**) into the word, it's fine just like it is. Let's look at some examples.

- Sandy practiced **her** song all day and night for the talent show.
- **Our** family sat in the front row.
- When Sandy sang, everyone covered **their** ears.
- Mr. Peterson, the judge, said **his** vote would not go to Sandy.

Contractions

Contractions are handy little words that are made when two commonly used words are smashed together—kind of like two train cars colliding and losing a little bit of freight. In the place of the missing letters, you need to put an apostrophe. The apostrophe shows the reader that you've held a space open for the letters just in case they want to come back.

There are a lot of contractions in the English language. Because there are so many, only ten common ones are listed. Do you know of any others? If so, take a moment to either add them to this list or add them to your notebook or spelling chart.

SHORT FORM	LONG FORM
they're	they are
can't	can not
shouldn't	should not
I'll	I will
you're	you are
it's	it has/it is
haven't	have not
we'll	we will
we're	we are
won't	will not*

*this is an irregular contraction

Did you notice which letters were missing in each contraction? What letter is most frequently dropped?

I'VE GOT TO RUN

It looks like this spy is in a hurry. Can you read what she wrote and count the contractions?*

> I couldn't stay.
> I've got to run.
> You'll find the
> jewel in the
> attic where we
> last saw it. It's not
> here because
> you're not
> likely to look.
> Don't forget we're
> Joe laid a top so
> shouldn't need to
> remind you we're
> partners!

*Hold this page up to a mirror.

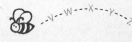

Contractions

Most contractions end with the words **will**, **are**, and **not**. Some examples are we'll (we will), they're (they are), and shouldn't (should not).

MISTAKES TO A-V-O-I-D

What's the Meaning?

Should not means "it's not a good idea," such as, "My mom said I **shouldn't** stay up past my bedtime." **Can not** means a person is not able to do something, as in, "I can't do a cartwheel." See if you can figure out which would be the correct words—or contraction—for this sentence: Joey _____ cross the street without permission. Now it's your turn. Try making up sentences using **can't** and **shouldn't**.

Now that you have a list of some common contractions, see if you can put them into a sentence or two. Which contractions might complete these sentences?

_____ almost ready to go to the park. _____ a nice day for hiking.

You _____ feed my dog pizza! _____ get sick if you do.

Gift Words

A compound word is made when two small words are combined to make one new word. Meatball is made up of the words meat and ball. Can you think of any other compound words that end with ball? Here's a hint: think about sports.

Punctuation Rules

The good thing about compound words is that they are almost all gift words. What does that mean? Well, if you already know how to spell the two small words that make up the compound, you'll be able to spell the compounds instantly!

Combine and Connect!

The following chart has starter words and choice words. For each row, there is a starter word and three choices to add to the end. If you want, you could think of these compounds as train cars. The starter is the engine, and one of the second words would be a train car.

Let's look at row number one. We have flag as the starter, then pole, ship, and stick. Therefore, the compound words would be flagpole, flagship, and flagstick. Hey, that's easy enough! Give the other lines a try. Write them down in your spelling notebook or chart. How many compound words are familiar to you? How many are new? Some of the lines at the bottom of the chart are blank. Can you fill them in?

Compounds to Go!

STARTER WORD	CHOICE ONE	CHOICE TWO	CHOICE THREE
flag	pole	ship	stick
nut	cracker	shell	meat
common	place	wealth	sense
rose	bud	wood	_____
table	top	cloth	_____
brain	wash	teaser	_____
head	gear	_____	_____
ear	ring	_____	_____
door	knob	_____	_____

Try This

Drawing Compounds

Get out your crayons and markers and see if you can illustrate the compound words! See if drawing a picture of each word will help you learn the word. Next, pick five words and add them to your chart of spelling words in progress. Which one do you think will be easiest for you to spell?

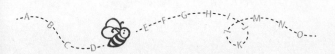
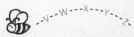

SHORT CUTS

This forest is very confusing. Only some of the words can be made into contractions; the rest can't. Color in the ones that can. Good luck!

he may

they are

they went

we will

do not

will not

we can

they will

she is

have not

has gotten

it is

I can

does not

does get

cannot

you can

TIGHTEN UP!

Contractions have been with us since ancient times. There are examples in ancient Greek. They show up in most languages.

Punctuation Rules

Now that you've tackled these compounds, did any of the words spur your imagination? Did you think of any other compound words that also begin with one of the starter words? Were you able to think of a compound word that ended with one of the train car words? If so, write them down!

Using Hyphens

Some compound words are two words combined but not exactly together. They have a hyphen connecting them. A hyphen is a punctuation mark that looks like this: -. In order to spell the hyphenated words correctly, you must remember to add the hyphen. Some examples are: **worn-out, mother-in-law,** and **life-size.** How do you know which compounds need a hyphen? The best way to decide whether a word needs a hyphen is to look up the word in the dictionary.

Paired Words

Paired words are pairs of words that go together but are not connected by a hyphen. Some examples are **post office, real estate, full moon, vice president,** and **Air Force.** Notice how the first word in the pair isn't just a descriptor, it plays a part in what the word means. If you took the first word in the pair away, it wouldn't mean the same thing. For example, you would go to the post office to mail a letter, but your mom or dad might go to the office to work. Can you think of any other paired words?

FUN FACT

Words Evolve

Words go from being two words to compound words in stages. The word **deadline** now means a date when something is due. During the Civil War, the **dead line** (two words) was the line the Confederate soldiers marked in the dirt for their prisoners. If the prisoners crossed that line, they would be shot dead. Through the years, it became **dead-line**, and now it's so common that it's one word.

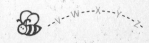

COMBUSTIBLE COMPOUNDS

Somebody has blown these compound words apart. Can you figure out how they go back together? One has been done for you.

berry

time

pine

dish

fire

straw

mouth

cup

port

butter

bed

washer

proof

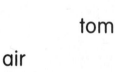

sea

loud

house

tom

gold

boat

air

apple

under

out

row

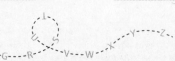

shell

boy

stroke

back

fish

stand

eye

lash

IT'S ALL IN A WORD OR TWO

The words that make up a compound word often have nothing to do with each other—like **court** and **ship**. Other times they are exactly what they sound like—like **newspaper**!

Chapter 5

A Word by Any Other Name

How Spelling and Meaning Go Together

Have you ever watched the movie *Akeelah and the Bee?* In it, Akeelah, a middle school student, prepares for the Scripps National Spelling Bee. She overcomes a variety of obstacles in order to advance to the national spelling contest. One lesson she learns is the importance of understanding the meanings of words. At first, Akeelah just wants to memorize the spelling of words. If you've ever studied for a spelling bee, you know this is almost an impossible task. There are thousands of words to learn for any spelling competition.

Akeelah's tutor, a very smart man, has another idea. He gives her lessons in Latin and Greek. He also encourages her to read great volumes of literature, so she can understand how the words are used in sentences. Akeelah thinks this is a waste of time. But the tutor doesn't give up. He encourages her to learn about the origins of words, and even asks her to explain the meanings of words only based on the books that she's read.

Of course, all this reading and writing takes a while, and Akeelah thinks it's all for the birds. She has a tough time grasping why these things are important until she is in Washington, D.C., at the famous bee. Then it all comes together. She's able to pinpoint each word's root, prefix, and suffix, and her studying helps her see how to spell those different parts of the word. Understanding the meanings of words helps her to spell any word—even words she's never seen before. Akeelah does very well in the National Spelling Bee, but just as importantly, she learns a lot of important lessons. One of them is that knowledge shouldn't be put into separate boxes. The things you learn for one purpose can easily be used in other parts of your life.

If you play a musical instrument, you know that being a fine musician doesn't just mean learning notes and playing them correctly. A very good musician knows how to play the

Greenburg Annual
Spelling Bee

melody in a way that will grab hold of the audience. The same holds true for sports. A good baseball player knows more than just how to catch baseballs. He knows how to work with other players, he can throw well, and he can react quickly to intense situations.

Back to Spelling

Good spellers must also be able to think, not just recite memorized words. But all is not lost! Most difficult words are made up of smaller words or simply have a prefix or suffix added to them.

Let's take the word **independence**. What prefixes and suffixes make up this word? First, there's the prefix **in**, which means **not**. On the other side of the word, you can find the suffix **ence**, which means **the state of**. Finally, we have the root word **depend**. Depend means to count on, or to need. Therefore, in•depend•ence means "to not be in the state of needing someone."

Super spellers at spelling bees ask for words in a sentence to help them understand meaning. Okay, it's time to give it a try.

The two-year-old did not like holding his mom's hand when he crossed the street, so he cried out for his independence.

That's kind of wordy. Can you think of a better word to use instead of independence?

Give It a Try

Now that you've seen an example of how to pull apart a word in order to figure out its parts, try to break up the following words and then put them in a defining sentence.

- encouragement
- disappearance
- unmanageable

Remember, break up the words into small parts first! Be a sight-word detective! Can you easily spot the root word in each big word? Now, here's the spelling part. With practice, do you think you will be able to learn how to spell the root words? For example, if you can remember how to spell **forget**, you will soon be able to spell **unforgettable**.

You're on Your Way!

Once you know the basic meanings of root words, you can understand a whole lot of words with little trouble. This knowledge is helpful with both reading and writing. You can amaze your friends when you are able to figure out the most confusing words in a book! You can impress your teacher when you are able to explain how you defined words. And, of course, you will be thrilled when your weekly spelling tests don't seem quite so difficult.

Grownups Need to Spell, Too

Being able to figure out the meaning of words is a helpful skill for grownups, too. Older students must know a variety of vocabulary words in order to do well on the SATs and ACTs, which are a big part of getting into college. Some of the vocabulary requirements can seem overwhelming if you are unfamiliar with some of the words. There are a lot of tough vocabulary words, but the good news is that breaking up words is not so hard to do.

Try This

What's the Origin?

Challenge yourself to find the origin of two or three unfamiliar words in the newspaper. In what country did the word originate?

A Word by Any Other Name

Let's see if you are smarter than the average high school college applicant. Can you take a guess at what the following words mean, based on your ability to break up words? Try breaking them into syllables and then find the root word, subject, and prefix and/or suffix?

- circumspect
- predispose
- unbridled

Let's Play a Game

Can you correct the following bold-faced words in this series of unfortunate sentences? The authors picked the wrong word to describe themselves!

- I feel that I would not be **invaluable** to any club I joined.
- People have said that my **idealistic** way of studying for geometry tests is **counterproductive**. You should try studying that way, too!
- It won't be **unnecessary** for me to try out for the cheerleading squad.

Did you see that for the first and third examples, the problem with each word was the prefix. Both **in** and **un** mean 'not.' So the first would make far more sense if it said, "I feel that I would be valuable to any club I joined." The third sentence just sounds strange. Perhaps, "It won't be necessary for me to try out for the cheerleading squad. For the second sentence, the author didn't understand what idealistic or counterproductive meant. Idealistic means you imagine the perfect way to do things; counterproductive means you make things harder for yourself! Don't forget to make sure you understand the meaning of the words you use in sentences.

Headline Headache

Stop the Presses!

Look at these actual headlines. Do you see how they can have multiple meanings?

Hospitals Are Sued by Seven Foot Doctors

Typhoon Rips Through Cemetery. Hundreds Dead.

 **61**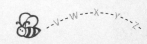

IS THAT AN ECHO?

Can you think of other words that sound like the ones here but mean something different and have different spellings? When you find the right word, fill in the correct sentence.

flower
here
sea
made
weak
one
brake
would
pour

I _____ with my eyes.

Once a _____ I visit my Grandma.

Careful with that vase or it will _____.

When you bake a cake you need _____.

If you have no money you are _____.

I _____ beautiful music.

Congratulations, you _____ the race!

That chair is made of _____.

Elaine works as a _____.

These four words have four different spellings, but they all sound the same!
right
wright
rite
write

Homonyms

Homonyms refer to words that share the same spelling but have completely different meanings. A **cap** is something fun to wear on top of your head, but **cap** can also be a verb that means to cut off or end. You might cap the number of people who can stand in a room.

Looking Closer at Homonyms

Because these words can be tricky, let's look at a few more examples of homonyms. Try thinking of sentences with each of these words.

- **bat and bat:** One is a wooden stick in baseball. The other is a furry, flying mammal.
- **dart and dart:** One is a seam in a piece of clothing. The other is a pointed instrument that is thrown at a bull's-eye. Have you ever played darts? If so, have you ever gotten a bull's-eye?
- **bug and bug:** One is an insect. The other can be a verb, meaning to bother other people. Here's a sentence that could be confusing for people who are just learning English: That bug is bugging me! Can you think of another sentence in which you can use both types of bug?

Homophones

There's an old joke that begins, "What's black and white and read all over?" The answer is, of course, the newspaper. One of the reasons this joke works so well is because it uses a homophone. This silly joke just doesn't have the same punch when it's written as it does when it is spoken, because the savvy speller knows right away that **read** refers to an action and not a

> ### Words to Know
>
> **homonym**
>
> The word homonym is Greek in origin. "Homo" means same, and "nym" means name.

Words to Know

homophone

Homophones are words that sound alike but are spelled differently. Just like with homonym, the "homo" in the word means "same." "Phone" means sound or voice. It's easy to remember because when you talk to your grandma on the phone, you listen to her.

color. This is not the case when the joke is told aloud to a group of friends! When you hear the joke told out loud, the listeners assume that the **read** is **red**, the color. This joke is a good example of the power of homophones in our language. Words that sound the same can definitely have different meanings!

Don't Be Tricked

Homophones are particularly tricky words. They can fool even the most careful spellers! They fool computer spell-checkers all the time, because the computer is only looking for words that are spelled wrong, not words that are used wrong in sentences. It is worth your time to look over the work carefully before you let anyone else read it. Obviously, it is important to be able to recognize which words are homophones and be on the lookout for them.

Pretest

Let's see what you already know. There are some homophones in these sentences that are used in completely wrong ways. Can you spot the mistakes?

My ant is write-handed.
She eight two many hot dogs and past home plate.

Know the Meaning

While it is not always necessary to know the definition of every word you need to spell, with homophones, knowing the definition is really important. Using the wrong word will create a glaring mistake and can even create some crazy, mixed-up sentences that might sound okay but read far differently! Here are some common homophones and their basic meanings.

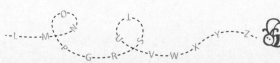

HUNDREDS OF HOMOPHONES

There are hundreds of homophones in English. Can you match the correct ones here?
Look out; there will be some left over because they don't all fit.

nun	sealing
wed	would
beat	none
grate	bawl
ceiling	bell
bald	hare
ball	here
selling	great
wood	boat
billed	beet
hair	greet
noon	build

ate	the past tense of eat
eight	a number between seven and nine
foul	a mistake in a sports game; for example, the batter hits a foul ball
fowl	another name for poultry or chicken
to	a preposition
two	a number between one and three
too	another word for also
deer	a forest animal, like Bambi
dear	a greeting at the beginning of a letter; also a pet name for someone
pail	a container; Jack and Jill ran up the hill to fetch one
pale	a faded color
sail	to float in a boat
sale	a time when stores drop their prices, like the day after Thanksgiving

MISTAKES TO A-V-O-I-D

To, Two, and ...Too

Of all the words that sound alike but have different spellings and meanings, two sets of words are probably the most common confusing sets. They are **to**, **two**, and **too**, and **there**, **they're**, and **their**. Take out your highlighter, and open up the newspaper. Now look for these homophones. Highlight them. You be the teacher or spell-checker. Did the editor use the correct homophone?

pause	to stop for a moment
paws	hands and feet of some animals (the singular form is paw)
hoarse	to lose your voice, or when your voice becomes scratchy and faint
horse	the animal
mail	something you receive in your post office box, like a letter
male	a man or boy, the opposite of a female
cereal	grains that you can mix with milk and eat in the morning
serial	a chain of events or stories that are linked together
there	an adverb, meaning a location
their	a possessive pronoun
they're	a contraction for **they are**
steal	to take without asking or paying
steel	a strong metal
ring	a piece of jewelry, usually made of metal, that you wear on a finger
wring	to squeeze out; you might **wring** a cloth or towel to remove extra water
flee	to run away quickly; a robber might **flee** the scene of a crime
flea	a tiny insect that likes dogs and cats; your pet might have a **flea** collar
great	something really good is **great**
grate	to shave, such as to **grate** cheese in the kitchen; also a frame with bars that's used to block an opening, such as a sewer **grate**
know	to understand
no	to refuse
hare	an animal similar to a rabbit
hair	something on the top of your head
read	the past tense of read; it means you have already looked over the written symbols and understood them
red	a bright primary color, popular for Valentine's Day

A Word by Any Other Name

die	the opposite of live
dye	to color or stain fabrics
ant	a small insect
aunt	the sister of your mom or dad
marry	to wed
Mary	a girl's name
merry	to be joyful or to have a good time
hear	to listen
here	to be in the place you are located
blew	the past tense of blow, like you **blew** out your birthday candles
blue	a primary color; the color of the sky on a sunny day
flour	a powder made from wheat that you bake with
flower	a blooming plant, such as a rose or a daisy
arc	a curved line
ark	a large boat
prey	dinner for a predator
pray	something you might do before a meal or at church
by	to be next to something
buy	to purchase something, such as gum at the drugstore
bye	a short way of telling someone goodbye
cent	a penny
sent	past tense of send
scent	a smell
fare	how much a bus or cab driver charges for a ride
fair	beautiful or balanced; it is also another word for a carnival or outside market
are	a linking verb
our	a possessive pronoun, showing ownership

"Aunt"   "Ant"

 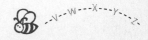

Mix It Up!

Sometimes it's fun to mix up words and their meanings. Think of a sentence using three of the words in the homonym list. Here's an example: **There are no deer in our yard.** Now, mix up the words with their homophones, so the sentence sounds the same but has a completely different meaning. Let's see. Now it would be: **They're are know dear in are yard.** Gosh, that doesn't make sense at all! How many crazy sentences can you think up?

Rewrite Headlines!

Grab a newspaper or magazine and look at the headlines. Rewrite the headlines using synonyms. What do you like better—the original headline or your version?

Check and Double Check

These days, almost everyone types on computers. Because computers can be so helpful, it can be tempting to let the them do all the spell-checking. But don't be fooled by the computer. While it is true that a computer's spell checker can certainly point out glaring errors, it won't fix any spelling errors with homophones. It's up to you to be sure that you've read everything carefully and checked for your mistakes.

Using the wrong homophone can lead to disastrous results! Imagine writing **You're ant scent you ate packages** when you meant to write **Your aunt sent you eight packages**. Now that would be really confusing!

Synonyms

Basically, a synonym is a word that means the same as another. You probably already know of quite a few words that mean the same thing as others. **Large**, **huge**, **big**, and **stupendous** are four words that mean the same thing. Why would you need to know such things when you are learning to spell? First, knowing a word's synonyms will help you understand the meaning of a word. Secondly, if you are writing and you are unsure of how to spell a word, you may want to exchange that tough word for a simpler word that means the same thing.

For example, perhaps you are writing about the Sahara Desert. Maybe you aren't sure how to spell the word **arid**, but you know it means hot and dry. You could use those simpler words that mean the same thing—and then go home and learn to spell arid! Remember, writing is a way of expressing yourself. If you can't communicate clearly, then people might not be able to understand you.

CINNAMON SYNONYM

Here's a fun game. Read what Sally is saying and see if you can pick the right synonym for each sentence.

My **MOM** likes to bake.
- aunt
- sister
- mother

I want to get a pet **PUPPY**.
- cat
- mouse
- dog

Let's go **TALK** to Ruth.
- shout
- speak
- yell

I can't get in; the door is **SHUT**.
- open
- ajar
- closed

It's a perfect day for a **RUN**.
- drive
- swim
- jog

I'm **STARVING!** Let's go eat!
- lazy
- thirsty
- hungry

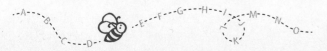 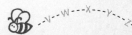

Tools Come in All Shapes and Sizes

Giving yourself a tool box of alternate words can be very handy. For example, if you were writing about a giant anteater, and you didn't know how to spell the word **voracious** but you knew it meant really hungry, you could substitute simpler words such as big, greedy, or even ravenous.

Practice Makes Perfect

Look at the following list. Can you think of at least one word that has the same meaning for every word on the list? The first one is done for you.

put	place
thief	_____
smart	_____
surprise	_____
happy	_____
pretty	_____
lonely	_____

Words to Know

unabridged dictionary

A dictionary that has not been shortened by leaving out terms or definitions. An unabridged dictionary is the biggest type of dictionary.

A Word by Any Other Name

Using the Dictionary and Thesaurus

Have you ever been told to go look something up in the dictionary to find out the correct spelling or pronunciation? That can be a difficult assignment when you don't know how to spell the word in first place! There are a few tricks to looking up words that can help a lot.

The dictionary and thesaurus are two reference books that can help you when you are trying to figure out the correct spelling or the meaning of a word. These reference books are usually available in most classrooms, libraries, and online. A dictionary contains a lot of really useful information. It lists multiple meanings for each word, which can be helpful if you're just not sure of the definition. The dictionary also has a pronunciation key and gives the origin of the word. Some children's dictionaries use pictures to help define the meanings of words. Other dictionaries, such as the *American Heritage Dictionary*, are unabridged. These volumes are very large, and you can find a lot of information about words. A thesaurus is a book that lists the synonyms of words instead of their definitions.

Three Steps to Success

Finding out information about a word you don't know how to spell in a dictionary might seem impossible, but there are three simple steps you can use to locate words. With practice, it can help you locate just about any word on your list.

1. Begin to think of the dictionary in four sections. Section 1 is the beginning of the alphabet, letters A-G. Section 2 is letters H-M. Section 3 is N-T, and Section 4 is U-Z. Take a few minutes to guess where the word you're looking up might be. Then open the dictionary to that section.

Play a Dictionary Game

Here's a fun game to give you practice using the dictionary. It takes two players. The first player will find an unfamiliar word for the other player to define. He writes that word on one side of a note card and the dictionary's definition on the other. Then he makes up two fake definitions. The second player needs to guess which definition is correct.

Words to Know

guide words

A pair of words at the top of each page of the dictionary. The first word in the pair is the first word on the page. The second word is the very last word on the page.

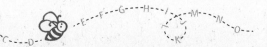

Try This

Alphabetizing

This is a good time to practice alphabetizing. Quickly knowing which letter comes before another is a valuable skill that will serve you well for years. To practice, take a pile of books and put them in alphabetical order by the author's last name. Next, put them in alphabetical order by the title of the book.

MISTAKES TO A-V-O-I-D

Smaller Can Be Better

Using the dictionary to locate spelling errors can be frustrating, especially when you are first starting to learn how to do it. Try starting with a smaller dictionary. A student dictionary will most likely have all the words you need to know, and it is much easier to use than a large dictionary.

2. Once you've gotten pretty good at opening the dictionary to the right section, it's time to tackle guide words. If you've been practicing alphabetizing, you should be able to quickly determine if the word you are looking for can be found on the open pages.

3. What to do if you just aren't sure of the spelling? Sound out the word as best you can. For example, if the word you are confused about is **producer**, maybe you're not sure if the letter after the d should be an e, a, or u. Concentrate on the first sounds of the word. Once you locate all the words that begin with **pro**, it should be relatively easy to find **producer**.

The Thesaurus

Roget's Thesaurus is a popular book for speakers and writers. Becoming familiar with this reference book will help you increase your vocabulary and help you find a whole bunch of different words that have the same meaning. Here's how to use it. The thesaurus is arranged alphabetically. Simply look up a word, then scan the entry to see what substitutions you could make.

First, examine a paragraph you've written. Highlight any boring words and any words you've used more than once (common words like **a**, **to**, and **of** don't count). Perhaps you wrote about your pet hamster, Max, and you wrote how Max eats his carrots. That doesn't sound very interesting or descriptive. Look up **eats** in the thesaurus. Now you can choose a substitute from an entire list of words! Maybe Max can **chew** or **munch**. Yes, your hungry hamster can sure do a lot more than just eat his vegetables. Obviously, a thesaurus can be a very beneficial tool. In addition to learning new words, you also have some new words to learn to spell.

A Word by Any Other Name

Have you become interested in crossword puzzles or word searches? Both of these activities are fun and helpful for many reasons. Crosswords help you with your spelling skills. Obviously, you would have a very difficult time fitting the correct words into boxes if you couldn't spell them correctly! Crossword puzzles can help you build your vocabulary, review parts of speech, and provide you with opportunities to practice using both the dictionary and the thesaurus. Word searches are super ways to review spelling words. There are a lot of books for both word searches and crossword puzzles, and you can also find them online. Of course, when you get to be a super crossword puzzler, you can always look forward to puzzles in newspapers. Who knows? Maybe you'll soon be able to complete the *New York Times* crossword puzzle every Sunday!

Be a Dictionary Detective!

Take one of the words in your spelling list and look it up. See how many flips of the pages you have to do in order to locate the correct word. Ten flips? Not bad! Seven? That's impressive! You might earn the title of Dictionary Detective if you can locate a word in five flips or less.

Try New Words

Get ready, get set, go! Rewrite the following sentence with an interesting substitution for **walk**: Whenever I go for a walk, something always goes wrong.

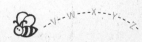

Chapter 6

When There Is More Than One

MISTAKES TO A-V-O-I-D

Singular Versus Plural

Be careful not to mix singular nouns with plural pronouns. In the sentence, "Everyone has their own lunch in the refrigerator," the word **everyone** does not go with **their**. That is because **everyone** is singular and **their** is plural. The correct sentence would be, "Everyone has his own lunch in the refrigerator." Unless, of course, you're speaking about all girls.

Plural Nouns: The Basics

Although nouns are pretty easy to identify—they are people, places, or things—spelling nouns is a whole different ball of wax. Spelling plural nouns can be especially tough because there are so many rules to learn. Sometimes there seems to be more exceptions than rules!

First Things First

Luckily, there are many nouns that only need one letter in order to become plural. That letter is, of course, the wonderful **s**. If you start looking at lists of words and highlighting nouns in books you read, you will discover that most words simply take an **s**.

Let's use items in a refrigerator as the examples. Here are some common (and not-so-common) items in both the singular and plural forms. By the way, this refrigerator sounds like it needs to be cleaned out!

SINGULAR	PLURAL
egg	eggs
apple	apples
a **jar** of mayonnaise	five **jars** of jam
one **stick** of margarine	four **sticks** of butter
one vanilla yogurt **cup**	three strawberry yogurt **cups**

Now it's your turn! Fill in the blanks to turn a singular noun into a plural noun!

olive _____

falcon _____

Not Done Yet!

You get the idea. But wait! There are usually many more items in refrigerators. Maybe there are **boxes** of juice! Lettuce **leaves**! **Tomatoes**! Maybe even a bag of ripe, red **cranberries**! There's most likely milk, too. But that's **milk**, not **milks**! None of these plurals will let you just add **s**. Things are not as neat and tidy in the fridge after all! It's time to move on and study the other types of plural nouns.

Nouns That End in S, Z, X, CH, or SH

These nouns are deceptively difficult. Making these nouns plural isn't hard at all. All you have to do is add **es**. So, going back into the messy refrigerator, we have:

- Two **boxes** of grape juice
- Three **bunches** of grapes

Nouns That End in Y

Nouns that end in **y** are a little more difficult to change from singular to plural because you have to think about that pesky **y** *and* the letter that comes before it. Be extra careful. If you misspell the singular form of a noun, then you could really mess up the plural form, too!

PLURALIFFIC!

It's more of a challenge, but it sure makes the language more interesting to have irregular plurals of nouns. Can you choose the correct endings here?

SHELF	shelfs	shelves	shelvs
DEER	deers	deeres	deer
CALF	calfs	calves	celf
MOUSE	moose	meese	mice
FOOT	foots	feet	fout
SHEEP	shoop	sheeps	sheep

Spelling Stories

Writing sentences or stories with spelling words can be fun. It lets you practice the word and be a little imaginative, too. Now, write two sentences that have these four words: **key**, **holiday**, **pay**, **monkey**. When you've created a super sentence, write it at the bottom of a piece of paper and illustrate the sentence up top.

MISTAKES TO A-V-O-I-D

The Apostrophe Trap

Make sure you read the sentence for meaning before you either add or forget to add an apostrophe. If the red strawberries in your fridge are moldy, you might refer to the mold as the **strawberries' mold**, not **strawberry's mold**. And you would most certainly not write, "The strawberry's are old and moldy." Now go throw those yucky strawberries away!

Vowels Count!

If the letter before the **y** is a vowel, then you simply add an **s** to the word to make it a plural. Think about the words **key** and **holiday**. The plural forms of these words are **keys** and **holidays**.

But Consonants Rule!

If the letter in front of the **y** is not a vowel, you must get rid of that **y**, replace it with an **i**, and add **es**.

SINGULAR	PLURAL
one **strawberry**	five **strawberries**
one **pansy**	two **pansies**
one **fairy**	three **fairies**

Look at the following chart and change the singular nouns into plural nouns. Decide whether you can leave the **y** the way it is or if you have to change it to **ies**.

thimbleberry _____

quarry _____

valley _____

fly _____

say _____

Nouns That End in Vowels

You have two choices for most words that end in vowels. You can add an **es** or just an **s**. Words such as **potato** and **tomato** will take an **es** to become plural. They become **tomatoes** and **potatoes**. Other words, like **piano** and **video**, only need an **s**. They become **pianos** and **videos**.

When There Is More Than One

Musical Instruments

This is a fun fact! All musical terms that end in an **o** become plural by adding only an **s**, never an **es**. **Piano** becomes **pianos**, **cello** becomes **cellos**, and a **soprano** singing a **solo** would become two **sopranos** singing **solos**!

Irregular Plurals

Some words don't want to follow any of the regular rules.

Words That End in F or FE

For words such as **knife** or **leaf**, you need to change the **f** to **ves** to make the word plural. One **leaf** will become a pile of **leaves**. The one **knife** on the butcher block might become two **knives** that need to be washed. Or **myself** might become **ourselves**. Here's an example: "I want to eat all the cookies today by myself. Tomorrow, we can make some more for ourselves."

Don't Change a Thing

The words **fish**, **moose**, and **deer** never change forms. If someone talks about his **fishes**, correct him, please.

What about Strange Things?

Every once in a while you might have the need to make capital letters, numbers, or even acronyms plural. To make numbers plural, you simply add an 's.' So if you were referring to someone who grew up when Ronald Reagan was president, you might say that he was a teen in the 1980s. To make a word like DVD plural, you would also just add 's.' You might have several Disney DVDs at home.

Words to Know

soprano

In music, a **soprano** is a singer who can reach the highest notes in a song. Maria Callas and Gail Gilmore are two well-known sopranos.

 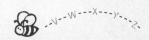

OH O!

There are two teams of nouns here, but they're mixed up. Some nouns ending in the letter o take –s as the plural, while others take –es. Can you see who's who?

RULE OF HMMM

In English spelling, if a rule is to work it must apply to a majority of words with few exceptions. Here's a good example: words ending with the letters f or fe can usually be changed to –ves in the plural, like **life** and **lives** or **wolf** and **wolves**. Can you think of more?

When There Is More Than One

Abstract Nouns

Abstract nouns aren't ever changed to plural because they aren't necessarily things; they're more like ideas. Honesty, courage, and respect are all abstract nouns. If someone were just learning English, she might have a difficult time understanding what these words mean. Write a paragraph about someone who you think is a shining example of an abstract noun. Perhaps you know a teacher or coach who demonstrates honesty.

One of a Kind

There are nouns that are so special you're just going to have to memorize their plural forms.

There is one common word that ends with **x** but doesn't require an **es** to make it plural. One **ox** turns into nine **oxen**.

There are a few plurals that deal with people that you'll just have to remember. The word **people** is the plural of **person**. **Men** is the plural of **man**, and **women** is the plural of **woman**. **Children** is the plural of **child**.

Words to Know

acronym

A word formed from the first letter of each word in a phrase, such as SCUBA (**S**elf-**C**ontained **U**nderwater **B**reathing **A**pparatus). Acronyms are different from other abbreviations because the acronym can be said as a word. USA is not an acronym, but SCUBA or NATO is.

abstract noun

These nouns are also called idea nouns, because they refer to an idea instead of a person, place, or thing. Some other abstract nouns are **bravery**, **trust**, and **relaxation**. The opposite of abstract nouns are concrete nouns. Concrete nouns can be noticed by one of your five senses.

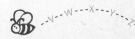

RED FLAGS

There are twelve flags on this page, and four of them having spelling mistakes. Can you see which is which?

Mouse

Mouse

Mouse

Mouse

Mloose

Torpedo

Terpedo

Torpedo

Torpedo

Mosquito

Mosquito

Mesquito

Mosquito

Formula

Formula

Formula

Fermula

Did you know the word *spell* has two completely different meanings? One is what this book is about and the other is how a witch makes magic happen.

Chapter 7

Capitalization Counts

Capitalizing on Capitalization

Capitalization rules in a spelling book? It may seem out of place, but knowing when to capitalize and when not to capitalize is an essential tool for super spellers. Not only will test-takers get these words wrong if they are not capitalized correctly, but mistakes in capitalization are as glaring as misspelling the simplest words. This chapter will highlight some of the most important capitalization rules and offer handy suggestions for navigating the capitalization corridor.

Names of People

Basically, most people's names get capitalized. These words are proper nouns, which identify specific people, places, and things. The pronoun **I** is always capitalized, too. But, like so many other spelling and grammar rules, this can get tricky.

Names in a Family

Capitalize names in a family when they are right before a name, like Aunt June, or when they are used in place of a name, like Dad. If you are speaking about a person in your family who you actually call Aunt, Dad, or Grandmother, for example, you would capitalize those words.

Grandma Mary is my favorite person because she always brings me candy when she visits. She and Grandpa Bob always come to our house for Christmas.

In these two sentences, both names for Grandma Mary and Grandpa Bob are capitalized because they are being treated as proper names.

Words to Know

proper noun

A special, specific person, place, or thing. Some examples are **Vermont**, **Mr. Carlson**, and **Kenwood Elementary School**. Your first and last names are also proper nouns.

common noun

Most nouns are common nouns. Common nouns refer to everyday people, places, or things. **Boat**, **umbrella**, **cat**, and **pizza** are all common nouns.

Somebody has forgotten to capitalize these words. Can you make out what the signs say?

A REAL PAL

A palindrome is a word that is spelled the same forwards and backwards, like **Bob** or **Madam**. Can you think of any more?

MISTAKES TO A-V-O-I-D

Pronoun Alert

If you're having trouble figuring out whether to capitalize the family member's name, look to see whether you are putting a possessive pronoun in front of the word. If you are using the words **my**, **his**, or **our** in front of the member's name, you would most likely not capitalize it.

However, if you are talking about a family member in a general way, you don't capitalize aunt, dad, or grandmother.

My dad can never crack an egg without breaking the yolk, but my mom says most dads can't.

Let's walk over to the senior center. A lot of people's grandparents live there.

You wouldn't capitalize the family members' names in these sentences because they weren't referring to the people as proper nouns.

Titles

When a person has a title, like sergeant or doctor, you would capitalize that title when you are referring to that person specifically.

Sergeant Miller is the toughest man I know.
Doctor Banks is the smartest doctor I know.
He's a lot younger than Pastor Grant.

In these sentences, both the title and the person's name is capitalized. The same rule that applies to family members applies to people with titles, too. If you're talking about these people in a general way, the words are not capitalized.

The sergeant is moving to Virginia.
I am going to the doctor.
I saw the pastor at the grocery store.

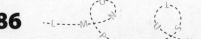

Capitalization Counts

There's a special trick to help you remember this rule. Just like a pronoun will let you know you don't need to capitalize a family member's name, an article (a, an, the) lets you know you don't have to capitalize someone's title.

Nationality

Because we're Americans, from the United States of America, we capitalize **Americans**. Always remember to capitalize the names of all countries and people from those countries. Here are some examples of countries to capitalize and the usual form of referring to their nationality.

Mexico	Mexican
Canada	Canadian
Sudan	Sudanese
Brazil	Brazilian
Russia	Russian
France	French

Religions

It's also important to remember to capitalize everyone's religious preference, too. Christianity, Judaism, Islam, and other regularly recognized religions are also capitalized.

States and Capitals and Holidays

All city and country names are always capitalized. Here is a double dose for you: a list of all fifty states and their capitals, all spelled correctly—and capitalized! Because it's a good way to organize them, they are all alphabetized.

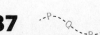

Try This

Pop Quiz

What do you call people from Switzerland, Egypt, Spain, Italy, and Japan? Pick one or two countries that haven't been listed yet and add them to your spelling chart to study. Don't forget to capitalize them!

MISTAKES TO A-V-O-I-D

Capitalizing Names

Don't forget to also capitalize deities, like God or Buddha, religious figures, such as Pope Benedict XVI, and holy books, such as the Torah and the Bible.

State	Capital	State	Capital
Alabama	Montgomery	Massachusetts	Boston
Alaska	Juneau	Michigan	Lansing
Arizona	Phoenix	Minnesota	St. Paul
Arkansas	Little Rock	Mississippi	Jackson
California	Sacramento	Missouri	Jefferson City
Colorado	Denver	Montana	Helena
Connecticut	Hartford	Nebraska	Lincoln
Delaware	Dover	Nevada	Carson City
Florida	Tallahassee	New Hampshire	Concord
Georgia	Atlanta	New Jersey	Trenton
Hawaii	Honolulu	New Mexico	Santa Fe
Idaho	Boise	New York	Albany
Illinois	Springfield	North Carolina	Raleigh
Indiana	Indianapolis	North Dakota	Bismarck
Iowa	Des Moines	Ohio	Columbus
Kansas	Topeka	Oklahoma	Oklahoma City
Kentucky	Frankfort	Oregon	Salem
Louisiana	Baton Rouge	Pennsylvania	Harrisburg
Maine	Augusta	Rhode Island	Providence
Maryland	Annapolis	South Carolina	Columbia
		South Dakota	Pierre
		Tennessee	Nashville
		Texas	Austin
		Utah	Salt Lake City
		Vermont	Montpelier
		Virginia	Richmond
		Washington	Olympia
		West Virginia	Charleston
		Wisconsin	Madison
		Wyoming	Cheyenne

Capitalization Counts

Celebrate!

Americans have many fun holidays to celebrate. These special days are capitalized. Here is a list of common holidays that are celebrated in the United States. Do you have a favorite holiday? Wouldn't it be fun if your birthday was a holiday, too? Everyone should get the day off on their birthday!

- New Year's Day
- Martin Luther King Jr Day
- Presidents' Day
- Valentine's Day
- Saint Patrick's Day
- Easter
- Memorial Day
- Independence Day
- Labor Day
- Halloween
- Thanksgiving
- Christmas

What are your favorite holidays? Do you like a special holiday that wasn't listed, such as Arbor Day? In your journal, try writing a sentence about your favorite holiday. Here's a sentence starter: My favorite holiday is _____ because _____. Take care to spell the holiday correctly.

More Days

And although nobody gets excited about Monday or even Tuesday, all days of the week are capitalized, too. So are months of the year. Add the days of the week and the months of the year to your spelling chart or notebook.

Try This

Pick a State

Pick two states, any two states, and concentrate on them for the week. Learn their spelling, their capitals, and one interesting fact about them.

MISTAKES TO A-V-O-I-D

Capitalize the Day

Did you notice that on some holidays the word **day** is also capitalized? Don't forget to capitalize both words in a holiday when you are writing about it.

MISTAKES TO A-V-O-I-D

What to Do with Seasons

Don't capitalize seasons. Spring, summer, fall, and winter are always lowercase unless they're at the beginning of a sentence.

 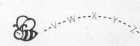

Try This

Design a Calendar

Create a calendar. Gather twelve sheets of paper, one for each month. On each, either make a grid or print out ready-made calendar pages on your computer. After you have your blank calendar grids ready to go, start filling them in. This activity will give you a lot of practice writing days of the week, months of the year, and holidays. Don't forget to add your birthday to the very important days!

Days of the Week
Sunday
Monday
Tuesday
Wednesday
Thursday
Friday
Saturday

Months of the Year
January
February
March
April
May
June
July
August
September
October
November
December

Here's an example that illustrates the rules of capitalization: The fourth Thursday in November is everyone's favorite fall holiday, Thanksgiving.

Geography Time

Like names of people, specific places are capitalized, but not the common references. So, Lake Huron would be capitalized because it names a specific Great Lake, but the word **lake** by itself would not be capitalized. This goes for rivers, oceans, mountain ranges, deserts, and glaciers. As you learn harder and harder words, you will probably need to learn how to spell the seven continents and five Great Lakes. They're listed here, but you can decide when you are up to the task of learning how to spell these big words.

Capitalization Counts

The Basics

Seven Continents	Five Oceans	Five Great Lakes
Africa	Antarctic Ocean	Lake Erie
Antarctica	Arctic Ocean	Lake Huron
Asia	Atlantic Ocean	Lake Michigan
Australia	Indian Ocean	Lake Ontario
Europe	Pacific Ocean	Lake Superior
North America		
South America		

Great Lakes

The Great Lakes are sometimes referred to as the inland seas. They have fresh water in them, not salt water like the oceans. Lake Superior is the largest and deepest of the five. The state of Michigan is surrounded on three sides by four of the lakes, which is why its nickname is the Great Lakes State.

Row Your Boat

Of course, we can't forget the major rivers of the United States. Here they are, in alphabetical order.

- Arkansas River
- Colorado River
- Columbia River
- Mississippi River
- Missouri River
- Ohio River
- Rio Grande River
- Sacramento River
- San Joaquin River
- Snake River

Capitalizing Publications

What do you do with books, magazines, movies, titles of songs, and works of art? Capitalize the first word in each one of these things! It's also standard form to capitalize each word in titles except for the articles—**a**, **an**, **the**. In addition, most prepositions that are written in the middle of titles, such as the words **at**, **of**, and **in**, are not capitalized.

Lots of Rivers Flow in America!

More than 800 rivers cross the continental United States. Most are small branches of larger rivers. What rivers are in your area? Put them on your spelling list and learn to spell them.

 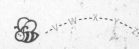

HELP THIEF!

This thief has mixed up all the capital letters and left them in a pile. Can you put them back in their correct places?

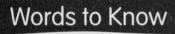

__hristopher __olumbus sailed across the __tlantic __cean from __pain in search of __ndia. __nstead he came to __orth __merica. __e brought three ships called the __ina, the __inta, and the __anta __aria.

Words to Know

preposition

Prepositions are words that connect nouns to other parts of a sentence. Some common prepositions are **over**, **in**, **among**, **at**, and **to**. Prepositions can also be more than one word; **next to** is one example.

Here are some titles:

- *Time*
- *Better Homes and Gardens*
- *Sports Illustrated for Kids*
- *Charlotte's Web*
- *Clifford, the Big Red Dog*
- *The Cat in the Hat*
- *Harry Potter and the Order of the Phoenix*
- *The Chronicles of Narnia: The Lion, the Witch, and the Wardrobe*
- *Mona Lisa*
- "The Star-Spangled Banner"

Let's look closely at the title of Dr. Seuss's *The Cat in the Hat* to make sure we understand what to capitalize and what not to. The first **the** is capitalized because it's the first word in

92

a title. But the words **in** and **the** are not capitalized because they're not the important words. See if you can break down *The Chronicles of Narnia: The Lion, the Witch, and the Wardrobe* and *Harry Potter and the Order of the Phoenix* or other titles in the series.

Quotations

Quotations are marked phrases that tell what people say. Usually, they are set off by quotation marks. You can find quotations and quotation marks everywhere. When a newspaper reporter interviews someone, she writes the person's words in quotation marks in the article so they will stand out. In novels, quotation marks are used to mark what characters are saying to each other. Why do you need to worry about quotation marks in a spelling book? Because capitalization counts in spelling, and there are a few rules you have to follow when you write quotations.

To Capitalize or Not

When you are writing dialogue or reporting what someone else is saying, pay close attention to the tag. If the tag, or describing word, is in the middle of a character's statement, then it is usually not capitalized because it doesn't start a new sentence. These rules can be confusing! Here are some examples of how to write dialogue.

Suzy said, "Please walk the dog, Jack."

The tag is at the beginning of a sentence. The **p** in **Please** is capitalized because it's the first thing she is saying.

"Suzy," Jack said, "will you come with me on the walk?"

Practice Makes Perfect

Write down five or six titles from various books in the library. Practice writing the titles, remembering to capitalize the right words. Next, practice giving titles to some of the writing you have done. Have you written a story you're particularly proud of? Give those stories some super titles! If you have only one-word titles, challenge yourself to use at least four words for each title.

MISTAKES TO A-V-O-I-D

Dialogue Tags

Don't forget to capitalize the first word of dialogue, even if it follows a dialogue tag. A dialogue tag is a word that describes how the dialogue is spoken. Tags are words such as **said**, **exclaimed**, or **asked**.

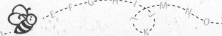

Try This

Dinner Reporter

Be a sneaky observer. Next time you are at the dinner table, try writing down what a few of your family members say. Then, work on spelling their words, and concentrate on capitalizing their sentences correctly. Who knows? Maybe you'll learn something new about your family that you didn't know before!

MISTAKES TO A-V-O-I-D

Quote Correctly

Make sure you don't put quotation marks around tag lines, such as **he said** or **she said**. If you aren't sure if you are writing quotations correctly, try saying what is in the quotation marks out loud.

This example has the tag line in the middle of the sentence. Because Jack is only calling out Suzy's name and then asking her a question, the **w** in **will** is not capitalized.

"I would love to go with you!" Suzy exclaimed. "However, I have to wash my hair."

In this example, Suzy is actually saying two different sentences. Because she is saying two complete thoughts, there are two complete sentences. But no matter what, things don't look too good for Jack, do they? I don't think washing her hair is a very good excuse; do you? Oh, well, thank goodness they are using good capitalization rules.

Letter Greetings and Closings

From time to time, everyone has to write letters. Written correspondence can make a grandmother smile, give best friends at camp a good laugh, or say "thank you" in a way that a phone call or e-mail never can. When you pack your bags to go to camp or on a vacation, don't forget to include envelopes you've already stamped and addressed to the people you want to write to. All you need to do is write a letter, pop it in the envelope, and send it off!

Friendly? Business?

Basically, there are two types of letters: business and friendly. The differences are pretty clear. Business letters are more formal. If there is an issue you care about, you can write a letter to your governor, senator, or representative. This type of letter is a business letter. Usually, when a person writes a

Capitalization Counts

formal letter, it is because he is doing work, or he doesn't know the person he is writing to very well.

You have much more freedom with friendly letters. You write friendly letters to your friends and family. You can write letters to thank them for a gift or just to say hello.

No Matter What

No matter whether you are writing a friendly letter or a business letter, specific parts of the letter should be capitalized and proper punctuation should be followed. Putting commas or periods in wrong places can make it very difficult for people to figure out what you are trying to say. However, when you follow basic capitalization rules, you can be as imaginative as possible and still be clearly understood. There are no guidelines for the length of a letter. It can be a few lines, or it can be pages and pages. What is the longest letter you've ever written? Do you enjoy getting mail? Maybe you could sit down and write someone a letter soon! But first, you should probably make sure you know the basic parts of a letter.

The Greeting

This part of the letter is what the reader of your note sees first! It can be fancy, with sesame seeds, or plain white and toasted. That is your call! The greeting of a letter does exactly what it says—it greets the recipient, or the person who is about to receive the letter. The greeting is always capitalized. **Dear John**. **Dear Dr. John**. **Dear Captain John**. In a business letter, you would need to put a colon after **John**. For a friendly letter, you would put a comma.

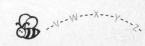

Parts of a Letter

There are three basic parts to every letter: the greeting, the body of the letter, and the closing. You could compare these parts to a hamburger. The greeting and closing are the buns, and the meat, cheese, lettuce, tomatoes, pickles, lettuce, mustard, and ketchup would be the body. Or, if you have a really short letter, you might just have bread and a small hamburger patty.

MISTAKES TO A-V-O-I-D

On and On and On

The body of a letter does not have to be just one paragraph. It can be as many paragraphs as you would like it to be!

Business letters are sometimes addressed to customer service representatives (the people you write to if you have a problem with something you bought, or if you want to thank someone for especially good service), and sometimes you don't know the name of the person you're writing to. In this case, it is common to use the standard phrase, **To Whom It May Concern**. That sounds pretty old-fashioned, don't you think? However, this nifty greeting is perfect in a lot of instances, especially if you are not sure who the reader is going to be. Notice how each word in this formal greeting is capitalized since it is all part of the greeting.

How would you begin a letter to some important people in your life? Would you call them **Dear**? Would you start out the letter with a **Hi**? Is there anyone to whom you could mail a To Whom It May Concern letter?

The Body of a Letter

Like a really delicious cheeseburger, the body of the letter is the good stuff. You can say whatever you want to, in whatever way you want to. It can be as large or small as you would like. Who could you write a long letter to? How about a very short letter, just a few lines? Whether your letter is chatty and full of fun or simple and to the point, you still need to watch your spelling, capitalization, and punctuation. Capitalize the first word of every sentence. Capitalize proper nouns.

Let's try it out. Get out some paper, go to Appendix A, find a word from the frequently misspelled list, and write someone a letter using that word. You don't have to send it off if you don't want to, but maybe there's someone you know right now who would love to receive a letter from you. Wouldn't it make their day to get a letter in their mailbox?

WRITE RIGHT

This pen pal is responding to a letter, but she's made some errors. Can you find five?

dear Mrs. Brown,

so nice to hear from you again. I hope your visit to doctor Wilson went well. I have to go see the Dentist next week and I am nervous because I have cavities. I'm going to go brush my teeth now. Please give my love to your cat felix.

Regards,
Betsy

HANDMADE WRITING

If you want to give someone a special gift, try a handwritten letter. A lot of people consider this a perfect gift because it shows you took the time and effort to think about them. Make it even nicer by decorating it with flowers or other drawings.

The Closing

Oh, the closing, the bottom half of the burger! Just like that bottom bun, it needs to be solid and substantial. If it is flimsy it won't hold up the rest of the burger and then you'll have a real mess on your hands! Most closings are comprised of only one or two words. These words are capitalized. So, the closing might be friendly, such as **Your Friend,** or really friendly, like **Love**. For business letters, the closing might be more business-like. You might use words such as **Sincerely** or **Very Sincerely**. Sometimes people like to write **With Warm Regards** or just a simple **Regards**. Finally, don't forget that the closing is the last bit of information your recipient sees. Try to make it fun and interesting.

Examples

Here are two examples. One is a formal letter, and the other is a friendly letter. See if you can notice the major differences between the two.

Capitalization Counts

To Whom It May Concern:

Yesterday I received your collar for my miniature dachshund, Suzy. Unfortunately, this collar was too large and she has been tripping over it! Did you not realize that miniature dachshunds have short legs? I need a new, Suzy-size collar fast. Therefore, I would like a complete refund as soon as possible.

I have enclosed the purchased collar as well as a picture of it on my dog. As you can clearly see, Suzy does not like how this collar fits her. Thank you for your prompt attention to this matter.

Sincerely,
Simon

Dear Grandma,

Mexico is so much fun! I am having a really good time on vacation, but I miss you and I wish you were here with us.

On Independence Day we went to Chichén Itzá, which was a major ancient Mayan city. There weren't any fireworks, but there was a light show that lit up the whole city. I'll show you pictures when we get back, but the best part was the huge pyramid. Liam and I wanted to climb it, but Dad wouldn't let us.

We're leaving on Saturday, so we have a few more days to enjoy the beach. Thank you for watching Fluffy while we're gone. I hope he's behaving himself!

Love,
Lily

Chapter 8

Testing . . . Testing . . . One, Two, Three

Oral Versus Written Tests

Many teachers give spelling tests once a week. This is a good way to see just how well you are learning your words. Let's look at a usual week of studying spelling. Mondays might be called Pretest Day. Your teacher will call out twenty words that you have never been quizzed on before and you have to try to spell them. At the end of the test you can see which words you got right and which words you need to practice more. Based on how you did, you can work on practice activities like the ones in this book. Later in the week, you might practice your spelling words with spelling dictation and oral spelling games and activities. This prepares you for the final test on Friday.

Spelling Dictation

Whether you are being tested in school or at home, spelling dictation can be a useful tool. In the middle of the week, your teacher or one of your parents will read out four or five sentences. Your job is to write them down with all the correct spelling and punctuation. Many times it is helpful to hear how a word is used in a sentence before you start to spell it.

If you want to try spelling dictation sentences at home, here are some tips. Make sure to include at least one spelling word in each sentence. For an extra challenge, always make sure you have at least one proper noun, one science or social studies fact, and some kind of punctuation rule. If you are practicing handwriting skills, try writing the sentences in cursive. It's also a good idea to start out spelling dictation slowly. Begin with one or two very short sentences until you get the hang of things. Spelling dictation prepares you for your future. Older students often have to write down information. They must be able to spell and punctuate that information correctly.

Try This

Try Spelling Dictation Now!

Give the following sentences your best try. Ask a parent or friend to read them out loud to you. And remember, everything counts!

* My dog Suzy likes her home in Columbus, Ohio.
* Do you know where Indiana's state capitol building is?
* Several states' capitals are located near Lake Erie.
* "New York City is called the Big Apple," said John.
* How did you do? Which one was hardest for you? What can you do to improve your dictation sentence practice?

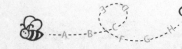

Testing . . . Testing . . . One, Two, Three

Oral Tests

You might learn best by hearing, or using your ears. You might be the kind of kid who loves to play instruments or listen to music. Maybe you can just think of the letters more easily when you don't have to worry about writing them down. If this is you, consider doing most of your studying this way. Ask your parents or friends to read the words out loud to you and then spell the word out loud yourself. Perhaps you might be able to test that way, too.

Making Your Own Spelling Dictation

Here's another way you can organize information for a spelling dictation test. Focus on spelling content. Here's a sampling of words with two-letter consonant sounds: **bang, beach, rang, ranch, rush, speech, throat, break, branch, path, shut**. Now here's a sample dictation sentence: **We shut the door, rushed down the path, and raced to the beach.**

Palindromes

Palindromes are words, phrases, or numbers that read the same both forward and backward. The words **did**, **dad**, and **mom** are all palindromes. Here's a famous palindrome that is a group of words: A man, a plan, a canal—Panama! Do you see how if you spell the phrase backward it will spell the same thing? Can you think of any one- or two-word palindromes?

SILLY SENTENCE

Some words are hard to spell. If you make a silly sentence
it will get easier. Try this: for every letter in the word SEPARATE,
make a list of words that turns into a silly sentence.

Susan Eats Peas And Radishes And Tasty Eggs

Here are some more. Can you make out what words these are?

Sam And Nathan Drank A Lemonade
Water Entered Into River Drive
Brian Attacked Little Lisa's Only Owl Nearby
Nine Inch Eels Cried Everywhere

**See if you can make up your own silly sentences from these
often misspelled words:**

fourth

occur

believe

Try to sing your silly sentences to
the tune of a favorite song to make
them even more memorable.

Spelling Counts

You can practice spelling when you are studying for other subjects. You probably have vocabulary words for subjects like social studies and science.

The Case of the Red Planet

Let's say you are studying Mars and you want to learn how to spell four words:

- Mars
- planet
- arid
- solar system

After you learn about the meanings of these four words and study them, try writing sentences using these words. For example, you might write, "Mars is a planet in our solar system. It is not gassy; it is arid and dry." Do you know even more about the planet Mars? Can you think of any better sentences with these four words?

Words to Know

anagrams

Anagrams are a type of word play. You rearrange the letters in a word to make a new word. The anagram for Mary is army. Do you see how both words use the letters **a, m, r,** and **y**? Some of the most clever and popular anagrams have words or phrases that have something to do with each other. Look at this example: **teach** and **cheat** are anagrams. Can you think of an anagram? It's hard, isn't it?

Try This

Four Topics, Four Words

Now it's your turn. Here are four topics. Can you think of four spelling words to go with each topic? Next, try to come up with four sentences with those words. Which words were difficult for you? Which ones were so easy that you could come up with more than just four spelling words?

- ✻ United States of America
- ✻ clouds
- ✻ chocolate
- ✻ ants

105

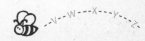

Words to Know

standardized assessment

If something is standardized, it means it's the same for everyone. An assessment is a way of measuring how good someone's skills or abilities are. In short, standardized assessment is a test! You can compare your scores with kids in other parts of your state or even other parts of the country.

Standardized Spelling Tests

So far in this book there has been a great deal of information about spelling. You've gone over various reasons you might want to be a super speller, a whole lot of rules, and a whole lot of exceptions to those rules. You've even learned many ways to memorize and learn words. But one thing that's hardly been mentioned something called standardized assessment.

Everyone Wants to Know

Any teacher can tell you that measuring growth in school is a fact of life. Though schools play many roles in a child's life, their main purpose is to educate and prepare children to be successful in their future. Tests that measure how well children learn are used to figure out whether a school is performing well, if a way of teaching works, or even if a teacher is doing her job.

For kids, the tests also measure how well they are doing. This is probably the most important group of all! Everyone wants to see the results of how he does in any activity, whether it is a video game, a tennis match, or the Iowa Test of Basic Skills.

Knowledge Is Powerful

Standardized tests can sound confusing and overwhelming. They can also be very helpful. If you never measure how well you are doing, then it is pretty difficult to celebrate when things are going well or buckle down and study when you need to improve. Even though no one actually enjoys taking standardized tests, it is an important life skill. Many professions require people to take certification tests. Lawyers must pass the bar exam, doctors must pass their medical board exams, and teachers must earn their teaching certificates and licenses.

It's Still Only One Test

No matter what, remember that tests only measure a part of
your abilities. All a test can tell you is how well you know some
information on one particular day. You might be sick or upset
about something, and that can affect how well you do. Take a
deep breath and do your best! That's really all you can do.

Getting Ready

Just like it is necessary to eat a good breakfast before you start
a busy, productive day, there are a number of things you can do
in order to do well on exam days.

Prepare

When you know you are about to take a test, there are
things you can easily do at home the night before to prepare.
Do some thinking about how you did in tests you've already
taken. If you did well, hooray for you! That's terrific! But if there
were areas where you could have improved, take a moment to
see where your trouble areas were. This is tough, but carefully
analyzing your pros and cons can sometimes give you all you
need in order to be more successful in the future.

Always a Brainy Speller

This phrase will remind you to do four things: **a**nalyze,
arrive early, **b**e comfortable, and **s**tay positive. The first step is
to review your past test results. See where your challenge areas
are so you can devote extra study time to them.

The second is to arrive early and be prepared. Have sharp-
ened pencils. If you forget a pencil, you might run around the
room in a panic, worrying about pencils instead of relaxing.

 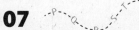 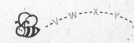

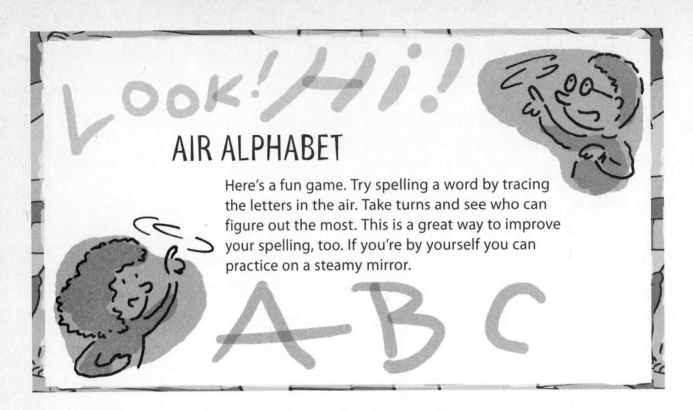

AIR ALPHABET

Here's a fun game. Try spelling a word by tracing the letters in the air. Take turns and see who can figure out the most. This is a great way to improve your spelling, too. If you're by yourself you can practice on a steamy mirror.

Third, one of the most important things to remember is to be comfortable. Some people have a really hard time with this! They get so worried about the test that they can't show everyone just how much they know! Do some little things to make yourself more comfortable. For instance, wear your favorite tennis shoes or your favorite shirt. Some people work best when they have a nice, clean desk. If it's possible, make sure your seat is away from other talkative people and your area is clean and gives you enough room to move around and think.

Finally, stay positive. If you continually tell yourself that you will do well, chances are you will. Have you ever tried this technique? This type of attitude helps professional and Olympic athletes. Many of them have said that they only focus on what they can do, not what they're worried about before a big game or match. You need to do the same before a test. Remind yourself that you've practiced and studied as much as you can. Picture yourself receiving a high score on the test, or a giant bright red 'A.' Last but not least, don't let people around you get you nervous or anxious. Those negative feelings can be contagious.

Testing . . . Testing . . . One, Two, Three

Test Time

When it's finally time to open up that test booklet, there are a couple more strategies to help you do as best as you can. The first tip might just be the most important.

Read the Directions

This is super important! Don't adopt a know-it-all attitude and forget to read what you're supposed to do. Are you supposed to circle the right answer? Write it down? Not write on the booklet at all and only fill in bubbles? Will you be looking for correctly spelled words? Misspelled words? Homonyms? Read the directions, and if necessary, read them again. One strategy that is very helpful is to let your fingers do the walking. Touch every word in the directions as you read it. By touching each word as you read silently, you will be forced to give each word your attention. Your directions will thank you for not skipping them!

CHECK SPELL CHECK

Morgan's spell check isn't working and he's made ten errors in this e-mail. Can you find the mistakes and correct them using the ten letters? Cross out each letter as you use it.

peelehuiaa

Hi Kim,

I went shoping at the mall yestirday and bought a new baseball glov. I'm realy excited to try it out. Do you want to meat at the field after sckool and throw the ball arownd? Bring your bat and envite the gang along. Meybe we can make it a regulir thing.

Talk soon,
Morgan

SPELLING GAMES

Although spelling bees originated in the United States, a British TV show called **The Spelling Bee** is believed to be the world's first televised game show. It appeared in 1938.

Testing . . . Testing . . . One, Two, Three

Answer What You Know

Some standardized tests are timed, and you have to make sure you don't take too long on certain questions. Even the most well-prepared test takers might come across a word or two that they don't know how to spell. In these cases, try using a couple of the strategies you learned earlier in this book. For example, does the prefix or suffix look familiar? Is the word a contraction or possessive pronoun? How is it used? If you can't figure out an answer to those questions and you still are stumped, mark the word and go back to it. After you mark it, move on and try to answer the questions you do know the answers to. Don't sit and stare at one word for a long time. That will waste a lot of time that you could spend answering questions you do know. Sometimes all you need is a little time away from a question. When you go back to it, the answer might seem more obvious.

Review

When you finish an exam, it might be very tempting to turn it in and forget it. But if you do have time, it's important to resist the urge to finish quickly. Go back to the beginning and review your test. The first thing you want to do is double-check that you answered every question. Now is the time to answer any questions you skipped the first time around. Make an educated guess for questions you are not sure of.

It might sound silly, but also make sure you finished the test. Sometimes test takers are so anxious to be done that they simply forget to turn over the last page and answer the last five questions.

Because reviewing is such an important test-taking skill, sometimes you find out some interesting things. Perhaps you misread the directions. Maybe you misread a word. For example, maybe in your nervousness, you read the word **though** as

through. That one little **r** makes a big difference! When you feel pretty sure that you did your best, then you can finally stop and declare that you've finished your test.

Take a Break

Test takers hardly ever get the results of their tests right away. After you're finished, there is truly nothing else you can do. Worrying about how you did on the examination will not help you or make your score better. Instead of worrying about the past, start thinking about some new information that you want to learn. There will be plenty of time to go back and revisit your test and analyze how you did at a later time. Once you're done, celebrate! You've done the best that you can, and that's all you can do.

Chapter 9

Just for Fun

Beano!

Bingo was originally called beano! Players would mark their cards with dried beans and then yell "beano!" when they won. But one day, someone got so excited that they accidentally yelled "bingo" instead of "beano." Not surprisingly, people liked the new name better!

MISTAKES TO A-V-O-I-D

Check Once, Check Twice

Don't forget to spell check! Sometimes it's so easy to get carried away with the game that you forget to check spelling.

Spelling Bingo

Do you like playing bingo? You can play bingo to win money or prizes, or as a fun way to learn information. You can also play bingo to help you learn how to spell new words.

Make Cards

The first thing you need to do to play spelling bingo is to make the bingo cards. Make simple grids on blank paper. They don't need to be very big, perhaps four squares going across and five squares going down. Four times five is twenty, so there will be twenty squares on your grid. Make the squares big enough so that you can write your spelling words inside them.

Playing the Game

Ask a few of your friends to join you, and have someone call out twenty spelling words. The spellers will need to randomly write the words in different squares without looking at each other's cards. Once everyone's grid is complete, it's time to play!

Instead of actually calling out the word, you'll get clues. For example, if one of the spelling words was **they're**, the clue might be, "This is the contraction for they and are." Or, if the spelling word was **Australia**, the hint might be, "This is the smallest continent." The bingo players will put down a marker, such as a dried bean or an M&M, when they hear the hint. The first person who fills in a line horizontally, vertically, or diagonally wins. Of course, they only win if they've spelled those words correctly!

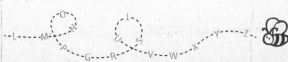

Just for Fun

Why Bingo Is Great

This game helps you practice writing your vocabulary words, and it helps you learn the definitions of the words. This is a great way to review homonyms and contractions. It's also a great activity when you are studying other topics, such as states. The clues could be the state capitals and you would have to mark the state.

Putting Words to Songs and Rhymes

There's a reason so many people can still remember the little rhyme, "i before e except after c." It makes sense, it is relatively easy to remember, and it is very useful. This is why it's such a good idea to try to spell words to a catchy rhythm, rap, or easy nursery rhyme, such as "Mary Had a Little Lamb."

Use Your Ears

Some people really enjoy movies because they can hear the action as well as see it. If you are that kind of person, give studying this way a try. You might be able to hear the correct spelling of words, and it might be easier than just reading the words. Kids who compete in spelling bees have to be able to listen and spell.

Have you ever had to learn to spell the seven continents? This can be a very tough assignment! Try spelling the continents to beats or to easy songs. Try spelling Australia to the tune of "Happy Birthday." Or, try this great little rhyme for the word Europe: E-U-R-O-P-E, Europe is the place to be.

Pretest Bingo

This is a great version to play with words you aren't familiar with. Fold a piece of paper four times to make sixteen boxes. Have someone call out sixteen words you haven't learned how to spell yet. You get an automatic bingo if you spell all the words in a row correctly.

Sing and Spell!

Here are a few easy songs to spell words to: "Happy Birthday," "Row, Row, Row Your Boat," "Twinkle, Twinkle Little Star," and "Doe, a Deer."

 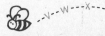

Worth Remembering

Even though those rhymes are pretty silly, they work for some spellers. In fact, once you can remember the spelling song, you might never forget how to spell the tough words. This is how a good rhyme can help a speller. Simple, good rhymes will allow spellers to concentrate on the word—just don't get too complicated.

Try This

Be a Magician!

Using a white crayon, write a spelling word on white construction paper. When you paint over the word with watercolors, the word will magically appear!

Using Your Other Senses

You've read about using your senses of sight and hearing to help you learn to spell. How about touch? That's right—feel those words! If you are the type of person who likes to learn by doing something, studying this way might be the best way for you. There are a lot of hands-on ways to spell words. One of the easiest involves a shoebox and a bag of playground sand that you can buy at a garden supply store.

ALIEN SOUNDS

These aliens speak phonetically. Can you figure out their message?

Peepul of Urth, bewair! We seek peese but will fite if nesesaree. Do not be afrayed of our youneeforms. Chews a gied to taik us to yor leeder!

Some experts say the English language is 85 percent phonetic. This means 15 percent of the words don't sound the way they are spelled. No wonder spelling can be difficult!

Just for Fun

Fill 'er Up!

To make a spelling sandbox, simply fill a shoebox with clean sand. Pat it down so it is fairly packed. Now try writing your name in the sand. Sometimes just the motion of your hand can help you learn. Imagine how much fun you could have practicing your words! If you mess up, you won't need an eraser. All you'll have to do is stir up the sand, smooth it out, and then try writing the word again.

Hopscotch Homework

If you enjoy writing spelling words in fun ways, how about creating a hopscotch spelling list? Using sidewalk chalk, make an interesting hopscotch grid on the sidewalk near your home, or on your driveway. Next, write each spelling word you are studying in the squares. Every time you hop, try spelling that word. If you get a word wrong, you'll need to go back to the beginning and start over again.

Try This — Beach Homework

If you're lucky enough to live near the ocean or lake, try writing your spelling words in the sand. Is there room for each one? You could even hop on each word and spell it out loud while it's covered by your foot.

Try This — Spelling Art

Using liquid glue, such as Elmer's, write down your spelling word. Now, cover it with glitter or rice. Buttons, old beads, and even tiny candies work well, too. You can use your imagination to make a beautiful word—maybe even one so pretty you'll want to display it in your room. Now that's a super way to look over your words before going to bed!

TRY A TRICK

To help with your spelling, give each word a personality of its own.

Imagine *desert* has only one S because it is dry and empty, and *dessert* has two because it is so rich. If you want to remember how to spell *principal* and *principle*, just remember that the principal is your pal.

Sometimes you can see smaller words in a big one. Put these small words together to form three big words.

GET HER TO

LOG CAT A

IN HABIT ANTS

Games to Practice

You can buy a lot of games to help you with spelling. *Sit and Spell*, *Scrabble*, and *Boggle* are all fun games that have been around for years. There's a reason for this! They are easy to learn, but they can be challenging for all ages of players and you can use them over and over again.

Don't Forget Technology

If you love to use the computer to learn, check out computer games and websites for fun spelling activities. Yahoo! and MSN both have a page for games, which includes some fun word games like Text Twist. You might be able to rent computer games from your library or school. Jumpstart, LeapFrog and Nintendo all offer fun kid-friendly computer and video games for spelling.

All in the Family

Here's a game that doesn't need any fancy batteries or gadgets. All it requires is an active mind and a few willing players. It's all about words that are all in the family, or that all have the same root word. Take a basic word, such as **play**. Now, see how many words you can come up with using that root word. For example, **play** can be found in **replay**, **plays**, and **player**. Another example might be **act**. Some family words for **act** are **react**, **active**, **acting**, and **actor**. You can play this game by yourself or with other people. If you play with other people, sit in a circle and take turns saying words. The first person who can't think of a word is out. Of course, since this is a spelling activity, don't forget to spell the words aloud as you name them!

The Scripps National Spelling Bee

The Scripps National Spelling Bee is the most famous and prestigious spelling bee in North America. It takes place every spring in Washington, D.C., and is even shown on ESPN. It is open to all students who are fifteen or younger (as of September 1) and who have not passed beyond the eighth grade.

The National Spelling Bee started back in 1925 with nine contestants. The *Louisville Courier-Journal* started the event. Later, in 1941, Scripps, a newspaper company, took over the sponsorship. There was no spelling bee during World War II.

How to Prepare and Enter

First, go to the Scripps website at *www.spellingbee.com*. There you will find all the information you need to know, including rules, study guides, and phone numbers and

Scripps National Spelling Bee

MISTAKES TO A-V-O-I-D

Remember the Rules

Many word families are made up of a variety of prefixes and suffixes. Don't forget to review your rules for adding suffixes when you create the families.

F U N F A C T

Time to Party!

Scripps Spelling Bee participants get to do far more than just spell during their visit to Washington, D.C. They may attend ice cream socials, barbecues, a talent show, and, of course, do some sightseeing.

WACKY WITCH

It's not just the spelling that's wrong in this scene. Can you see what else is wacky about this witch's house? There are five spelling mistakes and five things that are just plain wacky.

SINGLE STROKE

Letters that can be written in one stroke are: B, C, D, G, I, J, L, M, N, O, R, S, U, V, W, Z

addresses for the spelling sponsors for your area. In addition, ask your teacher or guidance counselor at your school for more information. Local sponsors work with elementary and middle schools to help the participants prepare for the bees.

Though steps might vary from community to community, usually students will compete in their school bee and move on to a local or city bee. Usually the top two or three spellers will compete in the regional events. On average, 250 spellers compete in the National Spelling Bee. Have you ever wanted to compete in a school, district, or national spelling bee?

How Do You Spell . . .

Here are some recent winning spelling words: guerdon (2008), serrefine (2007), ursprache (2006), appoggiatura (2005).

Bee . . . What?

What is a **bee**? A bee refers to a community in which friends and neighbors join together in a single activity, such as a sewing bee, a quilting bee, or a husking bee. The term **spelling bee** is an American term and first appeared in print way back in 1875. Usually, a spelling bee is an oral contest where spellers take turns spelling words out loud. Many elementary, middle, and high schools hold spelling bees. Winners from those bees will go on to compete in district, city, and state bees. The last step is the National Spelling Bee.

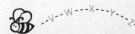

Everyday Spelling Lists

About the Lists

The lists are divided up into sections. There are between 50 and 100 words in each list, depending on the suggested grade level. Many of the words come from the standard list of the most common words in written English. You might notice that there is a great deal of variety in the difficulty of words for each grade level. It's that way on purpose. Spelling is guided by your ability to master words. Because learning to spell is based on different needs, each speller will find specific words more challenging than others. For example, one person might have difficulty learning the difference between 'our' and 'are,' while another speller might have a problem spelling words that have a blended consonant sound, such as 'blunt.'

Pick and Choose

You should choose which words to concentrate on. Take it slowly—only pick a few words to study at a time. You can also bring in your own words, either from the other subjects you're studying in school or from higher grade levels. There are lots of word lists here for you to examine. Pick the groupings that work well for you.

Because there are so many words and lists to choose from, think of a special way to mark your progress. If you are already using charts or notebooks, continue with that. Perhaps you'd like to highlight words as you master them. Maybe you even want to write the dates when you learned these new words next to each one. That way you'll really be able to see your progress. Some people like making flashcards and keeping the words in two separate shoeboxes, one for the words you know and one for the words you're still learning.

No matter how you decide to mark your progress, don't forget to take time to celebrate as you complete sections or master hard lists of words. Work with a spelling buddy and give each other high-fives for good grades. Buy a fun book of stickers to decorate your 100% tests. Maybe you could even make up some

fun coupons for yourself. Every time you master a list, you can earn a coupon for ice cream or some other fun reward.

Marvelous and Not-So-Marvelous Misspelled Words

At the end of this appendix, there's a list of some commonly misspelled words. You might want to pick and choose from these words when you are studying. Remember to use activities in this book to help you study words. Group spelling words in any way you see fit. The word lists are only guidelines. Last but not least, try not to get frustrated if you are having difficulty. Just like so many other things, spelling can be tough at times. But just because it's tough, it doesn't mean that you can't become terrific at it. Just be prepared to practice!

Try This

Snowman Spelling

This is a two-player game. The first player picks out a word from the frequently misspelled word list. Then she draws one line for each of the letters in the word, and a picture of a snowman. The other player guesses letters to fill in the blanks. Every time he guesses the wrong letter, a portion of the snowman will melt, or be erased.

First Grade

First grade is full of firsts. It's usually the first time you get to stay all day at school. It might also be the first time you get to eat lunch at school. Do you have a favorite first grade memory? Maybe it's learning how to read! Here are some common spelling words for first graders.

First Grade Spelling Words

the	he	are	as
me	this	of	for
was	on	you	from
and	with	his	they
at	I	a	be
map	cap	bat	have
to	when	with	want
cat	or	in	like
have	friend	mat	by
is	very	were	went
sat	one	you	about
my	she	had	that
said	house	us	we
not	it	home	dad
mom	her	but	

The EVERYTHING KIDS' S-p-e-l-l-i-n-g Book

Second Grade

Second grade is an exciting time. You are able to read even better, which opens up a whole new world. Second graders learn about their community and start to read lots of different kinds of books. Here are some spelling words to study at this grade level.

Second Grade Spelling Words

what	all	trace	when
there	because	were	land
pay	say	know	lay
may	too	ray	two
outside	inside	to	no
here	between	around	under
over	alone	a lot	went
plan	run	fun	sun
sister	brother	ran	can
an	which	their	said
fan	dog	cat	rat
fat			

Third Grade

There's a popular saying in elementary education. It goes like this: In kindergarten, first, and second grade, children learn to read. Beginning in third grade, they read to learn. Here are some spelling words with reading to learn in mind.

Third Grade Spelling Words

race	face	place
horse	meadows	our
favorite	really	always
finally	people	wished
own	most	queen
said	if	do
will	each	exclaim
how	up	out
them	then	many
some	so	these
would	could	should
other	into	has
more	like	make
take	than	first
been	its	down
only	use	eat
water	little	after
care	play	thank
subway	safe	asleep
spelling	east	west
north	south	

Appendix A

Fourth Grade

What do you want to learn in fourth grade? More science? More history? Maybe you want to become a writer.

Fourth Grade Spelling Words

words	called	just
where	almost	get
through	back	much
person	good	new
write	man	woman
around	another	came
come	because	different
again	number	between
along	while	might
next	sound	something
anything	together	important
animal	earth	that's
it's	we're	they're
can't	month	year
week	able	police
fruit	railway	pocket
attack	preschool	loop
shoot	booth	broom
mood	fooling	child
arrive	wounded	husband

Fifth Grade

Fifth grade is a year of growth for most students. Sometimes, this is the first year they change classes. In fifth grade, the spelling words can be difficult and challenging, and they often line up with the other subjects you're studying. However, there are still some general words that are a good starting point for spellers.

Fifth Grade Spelling Words

American	chapter	frozen
hamburger	companion	color
elder	ancestor	straighten
weather	aisle	lightning
talk	walked	wrinkled
wrong	foreign	chalk
habitat	solemn	absent
accident	government	migrant
present	resident	restaurant
statement	current	accident
knowledge	frostbitten	column
design	glisten	sword
participant	patient	pleasant
servant	continent	activity
advantage	balance	adventure
league	persistent	literature
inspiration	among	culture
creature	cassette	dictionary
persuaded	deceive	immature
legislature	furniture	type

  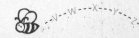

Challenge Words

Depending on how many words you have studied and mastered, you may be ready for some challenge words to really push your spelling abilities. This is the time to review some of the rules and study the suggestions in the book.

Challenge Spelling Words

activity	mitten	vacant
awkward	nickel	summer
feather	dollar	happiness
decide	proceed	collector
dishonest	treatment	attend
might	trouble	forever
music	winter	damage
dime	fear	distance
popular	source	exactly
toward	afternoon	mountain
double	fruit	quarter
windy	group	passenger
spiral	discover	reason
orange	devotion	single
advertisement	money	victory
exhale	penny	tidal
exist	partner	tornado
disappear	protect	citizen
delight	triple	

Outside Words

Here are some popular spelling words that have to do with things or activities outside.

Challenging Outside Words

county	boulder	volcano
island	thunder	geese
salmon	tornado	oxen
garden	geyser	harbor
raccoon	raspberry	forest
background	earth	
ground	dandelion	

Busy Words

Well, you certainly have been busy spelling words. Here are some more challenging words that have to do with being active.

smile	bounce	force
order	recruit	crisscross
count	adventure	destroyed
enjoying	sports	float
applause	repair	argue
drive	appointed	
hurry	picnic	

Appendix A

Frequently Misspelled Words

The following words are some of the most frequently misspelled words in the English language. Use the following lists however you like. Perhaps you want to study and practice them a few at a time. Or you might want to check first with a dictation test to see which ones you have trouble spelling. It might be helpful to copy these words onto a sheet of lined paper with a black marker. Laminate the sheets, then punch holes in the sheets and keep them in a binder. When it's time to do a quick check before turning in a paper or letter you'll be able to skim over your work, taking care to check these words. This would also be a great activity to do with a study partner. How do you think you will use this list?

Hard for Everyone

When you scan through the words, you will notice that they are listed alphabetically. These are words that people of all ages have difficulty with, so try not to be too hard on yourself if you have trouble mastering some of them. You're in good company! When you do notice you're having trouble with some words, see if you can find patterns in your mistakes. Do you have trouble with the suffixes? With vowel combinations? Are they difficult because they're just plain hard? Good spelling, and good luck!

Frequently Misspelled Words

accidentally	accomplish	achievement
across	address	advertisement
appearance	arctic	argument
athletic	attendance	balloon
barbecue	beggar	beginning
belief	biscuit	boundaries
business	calendar	camouflage
candidate	Caribbean	cemetery
changeable	characteristic	chief
choose	chose	clothes
colonel	column	committee
conscious	consistent	controlled
convenient	correlate	counselor
courteous	criticism	criticize
deceive	definitely	definition
describe	description	despair
desperate	develop	dictionary
dining	disappoint	discipline
disease	dissatisfied	dominant
easily	effect	efficiency
eighth	either	embarrass
encouragement	enemy	environment
especially	exaggerate	excellence
existence	experience	extremely
facsimile	familiar	fascinating
February	finally	fluorescent
foreign	formerly	foresee
forty	fourth	fulfill
fundamentally	gauge	generally
genius	governor	grammar
guarantee	guidance	handkerchief
happily	height	heroes
hoarse	hoping	horse

 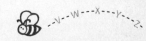

The EVERYTHING KIDS' S-p-e-l-l-i-n-g Book

More **Frequently Misspelled Words**

ideally	ignorance	imaginary
implement	incredible	independence
indicted	influential	information
insurance	interrupt	irresistible
island	jealousy	judicial
knowledge	kernel	later
latter	length	license
lieutenant	lightning	likely
loose	lose	losing
lovely	magazine	maintain
maneuver	marriage	mathematics
medicine	millennium	millionaire
minutes	misspelled	mortgage
mosquito	mysterious	naturally
necessary	neighbor	ninety
ninth	nowadays	nuisance
obstacle	occasion	occasionally
occurred	official	omit
opinion	opportunity	optimism
orchestra	outrageous	parallel
particular	pavilion	peaceable
perceive	performance	permanent
permitted	personal	personnel
physical	piece	planning
pleasant	possess	potato
possibility	prairie	prescription

primitive	probably	professor
psychology	questionnaire	quizzes
realize	really	receipt
recognize	recommend	referring
relieving	remembrance	reservoir
restaurant	ridiculous	roommate
safety	salary	scary
scenery	secretary	sentence
sergeant	severely	shining
siege	similar	sincerely
skiing	souvenir	stopped
strength	stubbornness	studying
succeed	success	surprise
suspicious	technical	temperamental
temperature	themselves	thorough
though	tomorrow	towards
truly	twelfth	unforgettable
unique	unnecessary	until
usable	usually	vacuum
village	villain	vision
virtue	warriors	weather
Wednesday	weird	wherever
whether	which	woman
worthwhile	writing	yacht
yield	young	

Memory Making

Throughout the book, you've encountered lots and lots of ways to practice spelling. These different ways should keep you from getting bored when you're studying and give you many, many opportunities to put your spelling words to good use. Now here are some useful memorization techniques that might come in handy, especially if all the fun activities don't help you as much as you'd like and you just need to remember how to spell that word!

Say It!

When you are forced to recite information out loud, your brain has to work harder. You also have to process the information more completely. Saying the word out loud will also prevent you from skipping words or letters by accident. Step one: Say the whole word aloud. Step two: Slowly spell the word out loud, taking care to really think about what you are saying.

Chunk It Up!

Chunking involves breaking up information into more reasonable and manageable groups. It is easier to recall small bits of information that is chunked, or grouped, than it is to recall a long string of information.

Use the word **Wednesday** as your example. It's easier to break up Wednesday into three chunks than to remember all nine letters at a time. To spell Wednesday correctly, you just need to remember **Wed**, then **nes**, and finally **day**. These chunks are each three letters long and may be already words you know how to spell. That's a lot easier than remembering to say **W-e-d-n-e-s-d-a-y**. Now tackle **Saturday**. How would you chunk this day of the week?

Mnemonic Devices

Talk about a difficult word for something fun to do! Mnemonic devices are phrases that can help you recall large amounts of information. Mnemonic devices are especially useful in science or social studies classes because you usually have to remember a lot of lists.

Music students often learn the mnemonic **Every Good Boy Does Fine**. That stands for the lines on the treble clef: E, G, B, D, F. Mnemonic devices work for spelling words, too. Here's a hint for the word **field**: **Father, Is Every Lake Deep?** Okay, obviously the device has nothing to do with the meaning of the word, but it does have a word for each letter of field. It's kind of fun to think of crazy sentences, especially if they are helpful!

You give it a try now. For the following words, see if you can come up with a fun and interesting mnemonic device. Can't do fun or interesting? Okay. How about a sentence or question that makes sense.

 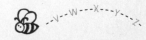

- balloon _____

- genius _____

- heroes _____

- twelfth _____

What did you come up with? Do you think this method will help you remember how to spell the words? Why or why not?

Link It Up!

When mnemonic devices fail to trigger your memory, try visualization. What you do is link up information you want to remember with a visual picture. Then all you have to do is remember the picture in your mind in order to recall facts. Try linking with the spelling word **balloon**. The reason it is labeled as a frequently misspelled word is that people forget to include two 'Ls' and two 'Os' in it.

To begin, think about how balloons float in the sky. Imagine two balloons floating side by side in a beautiful summer sky. Those two floating balloons could stand for the two 'Ls' and the two 'Os' in the spelling word. Linking might be a difficult undertaking for a list of twenty words. But if there's just one word in particular that is giving you trouble, remembering how to spell it with visual clues might be incredibly helpful.

Concentrate!

The other day a girl was reading a recipe, watching the news, and talking with members of her family as they walked into the kitchen. Because of everything that was going on around her, she misread the ingredient list and put way too much flour in her cake recipe. The cake didn't turn out well. The layers weren't light and fluffy; they were more like layers of bricks! This little story shows you how easy it is to get caught up in doing more than one thing at a time. If you're doing your best to commit difficult words to memory, you need to give yourself some quiet time in which to study. Try giving yourself some spelling time.

Where do you study best? At the kitchen or dining room table? On the floor in the den? At your desk in your room? On your bed? When do you concentrate the best? In the morning? As soon as you get home from school? After dinner? Do you like to be alone? With other people? Once you've learned what your ideal study situation is, it will be easier for you to be able to concentrate. When you do sit down to study or work on spelling projects, do so with a purpose.

Give yourself some goals when you sit down to study. Perhaps you want to be able to spell five words in the next fifteen minutes. Maybe you're going to need thirty minutes. Maybe you only want to concentrate on two or three words at a time. Maybe you want to look at the whole list of twenty words. No matter what you decided, stick to your goal. Concentrate on that one task and see if it makes a difference.

The Four Rs

Finally, when you are working on keys to memorization, it's a good idea to remember the four Rs. People used to say that the three Rs were reading, writing, and arithmetic. Don't you think that's kind of funny? After all, neither **writing** nor **arithmetic** begin with an **r**. Anyway, in order to memorize information well, you can put four things into practice. This process sounds like it will take a very long time, but actually, it doesn't take long at all once you get the hang of it.

1. **Read** the word you are hoping to study carefully. That's easy enough!
2. **Reflect** on the word. To reflect means to think seriously about something. When you reflect on how a word is spelled, you need to study it carefully. For example, perhaps you are studying the word **yield**. Yield follows the famous rule, **i** before **e** except after **c**. You know that the two vowels in the word are **ie**. Now whenever you think about spelling **yield**, you will need to reflect on how it is an example of spelling a word with the **i** before the **e**.
3. **Recite** the word out loud. It's a fairly easy word to spell because it doesn't have too many letters. Spell it out loud again. Now you might want to go on to the next word you are studying and go through the same process of reading, reflecting, and reciting.

4. **Review** all of your words. To review means to look over, study, or examine again. That's exactly what you'll need to do when you study your spelling words! Review the spelling of **yield** again. Perhaps you can even try to think if yield is spelled the same as another word you might already know, such as **field**. After doing all of that, do you know the word any better?

Words to Know

word traps

Some words are definitely traps for super spellers! Many words have multiple meanings, and some words in our language just don't make sense at all. Otherwise, a pineapple would have something to do with apples, right? Or a boxing ring wouldn't be square! Watch out for these traps!

Appendix B

Resources

Books

Webster's Dictionary. (Merriam-Webster, July 2004)
This dictionary is hardcover and easy to use.

Unabridged Dictionary, Second Edition. (Random House Reference, July 2005)
An unabridged dictionary is essential when you are looking up root words and the origin of words. This version is fairly easy to read and is not as expensive as many others on the market.

Scholastic Children's Dictionary. (Scholastic Reference, Revised, June 2007)
This dictionary is colorful and fun. There are a lot of illustrations and the text is large.

Scholastic Dictionary of Spelling. (Scholastic Reference, Revised, July 2006)
This book is paperback and is yet another handy tool if you're struggling to improve your spelling.

The American Heritage Children's Thesaurus. (Houghton Mifflin, Updated Edition, May 2006)
This book is a great beginner's thesaurus. It's has 4,000 entries and 36,000 synonyms. The font is big enough that you can find words easily.

Roget's International Thesaurus. (Collins, 6th Revised Edition, July 2002)
What makes this thesaurus so many people's favorite is that the words are grouped by content. If you look up **happy**, you will find all kinds of words that will mean just that.

25 Super-Fun Spelling Games (Leber, Scholastic, 1999)
Here's a list of many more games and ideas to make spelling fun.

Appendix B

The Big Book of Spelling Tests. (Hargraves, Black Dog and Levental Publishers, Spiral Edition, June 2007)
The interesting thing about this book is that the author gives you spelling tests in a variety of formats. He gives multiple choice and fill-in-the-blank tests. These formats will help in preparation for any standardized spelling test.

How to Spell Like a Champ. (Tinkle, Andrews, Kimple. Workman Publishing Company, October 2006)
The authors are former spelling bee champions. Throughout the book, they give tips and strategies for anyone who wants to seriously compete in the Scripps National Spelling Bee.

DVDs

The Best of the National Spelling Bee (ESPN, November 2006)
This movie highlights some of the best moments in the national spelling bee.

Akeelah and the Bee (Lions Gate, August 2006)
This movie is a favorite spelling bee movie because it really shows how dedicated the spelling bee participants and their many coaches are.

Spellbound (Sony Pictures, January 2004)
This movie is a documentary. It follows the journey of eight teenagers in their quest to go to the Scripps National Spelling Bee.

Games

Scrabble (Hasbro)
This game is available in a large number of editions, from travel editions to super-deluxe editions with boards that can turn. The basic game involves trying to score as many points as possible by forming words. However, the possibilities for using this game to help with spelling are endless.

Boggle (Hasbro)
This popular game involves shaking up lettered cubes, dropping them in a grid, setting a timer, and then racing to see who can come up with the most words. This game is very useful as a fun, relaxing way of keeping spelling skills up-to-date.

Boggle Junior Letters (Hasbro)
This game helps children learn letters, learn to spell, and learn to read. It uses pictures and matching games. It's a great first spelling game.

Websites

Scripps National Spelling Bee
This site tells you everything you need to know about the National Spelling Bee.
www.spellingbee.com

Commonly Misspelled Words
Here's one of the many sites to locate commonly misspelled words.
www.esldesk.com

 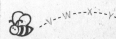

Appendix C

Puzzle Answers

CHAPTER 1
page 3 ✳ **Better Letter**

In the word **stack** change one letter to describe a piece of celery. **STALK**

Change an r in **order** to describe somebody who is not as young as you. **OLDER**

Replace one letter in **song** to describe something that is not short. **LONG**

Replace the double letters to make **berry** something everyone has. **BELLY**

Change a letter in **hike** to describe something you enjoy. **LIKE**

Change one letter in **decay** to describe something that makes you wait. **DELAY**

If you change one letter in **foot**, you get somebody acting silly. **FOOL**

page 9 ✳ **Follow the Line**

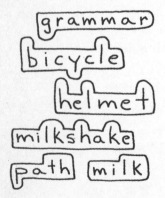

page 13 ✳ **Off to Spell**

school

CHAPTER 2
page 20 ✳ **Goodbye, Eee!**

There are many words that lose the letter e when —ing is added. Here are just a few of them:

come	coming	leave	leaving
take	taking	evade	evading
organize	organizing	sue	suing
taste	tasting	make	making
chime	chiming	close	closing

page 23 ✳ **Wise as an Owl**

greatful = grateful

fourty = forty

decieve = deceive

beleive = believe

fungis = fungus

pengiun = penguin

roomate = roommate

definite = definite

slowlie = slowly

page 25 ✳ **The Long Way**

grape

trade

green

tree

bike

right

row

rope

ruler

pure

page 27 ✳ **Prefix This**

b. impolite

c. unwrap

c. draw it again

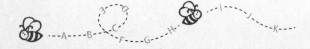 

Appendix C

CHAPTER 3
page 33 ✳ **Various Verbs**

put   bid   split   spread

page 36 ✳ **Lazy Letters**

irregular   alphabet   pronounce
definition   orginal

page 39 ✳ **Latin Scramble**

domestic — found at home

dictate — to read aloud

transit — to pass over or across

pacific — the largest ocean

alien — not from here

page 42 ✳ **From the Spanish**

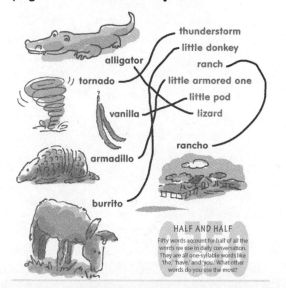

alligator — lizard

tornado — thunderstorm

vanilla — little pod

armadillo — little armored one

burrito — little donkey

rancho — ranch

HALF AND HALF
Fifty words account for half of all the words we use in daily conversation. They are all one-syllable words like 'the,' 'have,' and 'you.' What other words do you use the most?

CHAPTER 4
page 49 ✳ **Mine and Yours**

The following sentences have possessive nouns:
That boy's skateboard is green.
My mother's apron is missing.
The cat's tail is twitching.
The girl's journal is full of writing.

page 51 ✳ **I've Got to Run**

I cOuldn't Stay,
I'vE goT to rUN.
You'll FinD tHe
jEwels iN The
aTtic WhEre
we'D agreed
he's not likely
To lOok.
DoN't forget
we've gOt a
DeAl so I
shouldn't have
to reMind
yOu we'Re
pArtnErs!

There are 9 contractions.

page 54 ✳ **Short Cuts**

they are	they're	she is	she's
we will	we'll	have not	haven't
do not	don't	it is	it's
will not	won't	does not	doesn't
they will	they'll	cannot	can't

 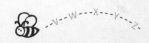

The EVERYTHING KIDS' S-p-e-l-l-i-n-g Book

page 56 ✳ **Combustible Compounds**

pineapple	airport	seashell
buttercup	backstroke	strawberry
rowboat	fireproof	tomboy
outhouse	goldfish	dishwasher
understand	bedtime	eyelash
loudmouth		

CHAPTER 5
page 62 ✳ **Is That an Echo?**

I SEE with my eyes
Once a WEEK I visit my grandma
Careful with that vase or it will BREAK.
When you bake a cake you need FLOUR.
If you have no money you are POOR.
I HEAR beautiful music.
Congratulations, you WON the race!
That chair is made of WOOD.
Elaine works as a MAID.

page 65 ✳ **Hundreds of Homophones**

beat, beet	grate, great
ceiling, sealing	ball, bawl
wood, would	billed, build
hair, hare	nun, none

page 69 ✳ **Cinnamon Synonym**

My MOM likes to bake. The synonym is MOTHER.
I want to get a PUPPY. The synonym is DOG.
Let's go TALK to Ruth. The synonym is SPEAK.
I can't get in; the door is SHUT. The synonym is CLOSED.
It's a perfect day for a RUN. The synonym is JOG.
I'm STARVING! Let's go eat! The synonym is HUNGRY.

CHAPTER 6
page 77 ✳ **Pluraliffic**

SHELF	shelves
DEER	deer
CALF	calves
MOUSE	mice
FOOT	feet
SHEEP	sheep

page 80 ✳ **Oh O!**

autos echoes heroes zoos

photos pianos tomatoes torpedoes

memos volcanoes tattoos potatoes

Appendix C

page 82 ✳ **Red Flags**

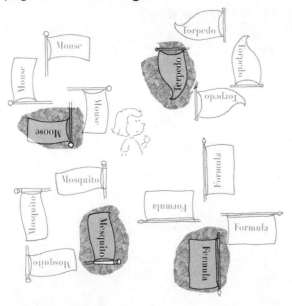

CHAPTER 7
page 85 ✳ **Spiral Spelling**

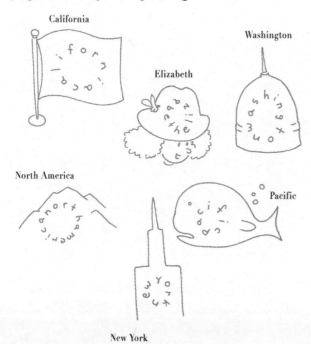

California

Washington

Elizabeth

North America

Pacific

New York

page 92 ✳ **Help Thief!**

Christopher Columbus sailed across the Atlantic Ocean from Spain in search of India. Instead he came to North America. He brought three ships called the Nina, the Pinta, and the Santa Maria.

page 97 ✳ **Write Right**

Dear Mrs. Brown,

So nice to hear from you again. I hope your visit to Doctor Wilson went well. I have to go see the dentist next week and I am nervous because I have cavities. I'm going to go brush my teeth now. Please give my love to your cat Felix.

Regards,
Betsy

CHAPTER 8
page 104 ✳ **Silly Sentence**

Sam And Nathan Drank A Lemonade
Water Entered Into River Drive
Brian Attacked Little Lisa's Only Owl Nearby
Nine Inch Eels Cried Everywhere

SANDAL
WEIRD
BALLOON
NIECE

page 110 ✳ **Check Spell Check**

Hi Kim,
I went shopping at the mall yesterday and bought a new baseball glove. I'm really excited to try it out. Do you want to meet at the field after school and throw the ball around? Bring your bat and invite the gang along.
Maybe we can make it a regular thing.
Talk soon,
Morgan

  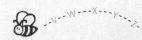